Lucinda Green (née Prior-Palmer), MBE, began riding at the age of four. She entered the event world at sixteen years of age with her first horse, Be Fair, and a year later they had earned a place in the British Junior European Team. At the age of nineteen, Lucinda and Be Fair won Badminton together and competed in Kiev as members of the Senior European Team. At twenty-one, Lucinda and Be Fair became the Individual European Champions. The success story continued with different horses and in 1977 Lucinda achieved the distinction of being the first to have won the European Championships twice and to have won Badminton and Burghley in the same year. Two years later, riding Killaire, Lucinda claimed the Whitbread Trophy and thereby set a record for having won Badminton four times on four different horses. In 1980 Beagle Bay gave Lucinda her second win at Burghley.

In September 1982 Lucinda and Regal Realm gained the highest prize the sport has to offer when they deservedly won the World Championships in Luhmühlen. Seven months later they confirmed their supremacy by winning Badminton – which gave Lucinda her record fifth victory there within a decade. In 1983 she won the individual and team silver medals with Regal Realm at the European Championships in Frauenfeld, Switzerland, and 1984 saw a record-breaking sixth win at Badminton with Beagle Bay and the winning of the team silver medal with Regal Realm at the Los Angeles Olympic Games.

Lucinda Green is also a regular and popular contributor to *Riding* magazine.

The pictures on the front cover show (clockwise from top left): Killaire in the dressage phase at Badminton in 1980 (*Kit Houghton*), Wide Awake at the Normandy Bank, Badminton, in 1976, George show-jumping at Burghley in 1977 and Be Fair at Osberton in 1973, the year he won Badminton (*Marston Photographics*). The picture on the back shows Killaire and Lucinda with the Whitbread Trophy in 1979 (*Kit Houghton*).

By the same author

UP, UP AND AWAY: The biography of Be Fair
REGAL REALM: A World Champion's story

LUCINDA GREEN

Four Square

A TRIBUTE TO
BE FAIR, WIDE AWAKE,
GEORGE and KILLAIRE

Methuen · London

A Methuen Paperback

First published in Great Britain 1980
by Pelham Books Ltd
This edition first published in 1985
by Methuen London Ltd
11 New Fetter Lane, London EC4P 4EE

© 1980, 1985 Lucinda Green (née Prior-Palmer)
(by permission of the
British Equestrian Federation,
to whom a donation has been made)

ISBN 0 413 55610 7

Printed in Great Britain
by Hazell Watson & Viney Ltd
Member of the BPCC Group
Aylesbury, Bucks

To My Mother

Contents

List of Illustrations

Acknowledgements

To Charles Cyzer, Vicki Phillips and
Elaine Straker for allowing me to ride
their precious horses; to them and their
connections for their help in supplying
information about their horses.

To Joanna Capjon and Lisa Waltman
for their unlimited dedication to the Four
and for the information they provided.

To Anna Collins and Barbara Cooper
who permitted me to re-use a chapter
originally written for the book *Burghley*.

To Joss and Rosalind Hanbury and to
Chris and Susanne Collins who provided
hospitality and shelter at the inspiring
and beautiful 'Burley-on-the-Hill', where
this book was written.

To my family, Eric Marriott, Lesley
Gowers and Michael Sissons, for their
consistent tolerance and encouragement
during this, a second manuscript.

To Jane Starkey, Michele Price and
Emma Murdoch, all three of whom
shared the labour of typing the
manuscript at great speed from badly
recorded tapes.

Special Acknowledgements

To Bob Dean and British Equestrian Promotions, to Jack Reynolds and the British Equestrian Federation, to David Kingsley and to Colonel Bill Lithgow for the support they give to the sport and to myself.

To the sport's principal sponsors, The Midland Bank, Whitbread and Raleigh and to Overseas Containers Ltd.

To all those kind and hard-working people who rarely receive personal acknowledgement but without whom there would be no competitions and no story of the Four. The British Horse Society, landowners, fence judges, course-builders, car-park attendants, St John Ambulance and Red Cross, arena parties, scorers, secretaries and organisers, are but a few of those to whom I would like to extend my warmest thanks.

Preface

This book is written in
enthusiasm for and admiration of
four bold, generous horses.
Their separate stories
are told from one viewpoint
and must surely leave
much unsaid and many,
including fellow competitors,
unmentioned. I apologise –
but that would be another book.

Four Square

One

Sir Victor Sassoon bred and owned four Derby winners between 1953 and 1960. He commemorated such fortune in an original manner: small paintings of each horse were placed four square under the glass in the centre of a tray.

This book, although a less original idea, is produced twenty years later with similar intentions. It is a tribute from their rider to four great horses in another sphere: Be Fair, Wide Awake, George and Killaire. In the seven years from 1973 to 1979, each of these horses won the world's greatest three-day horse trials – Badminton – and two, Be Fair and George, followed this by winning the European Championships.

The questions often raised are, 'What makes a Badminton winner? What do the four have in common?' Finding the right horse, as many will know, is one of the hardest parts of equestrian sport, especially in a branch of the sport where no particular blood-line has built itself a reputation. In a great many cases the right horse has come by accident. In my case, four accidents.

After Badminton 1979, Loriner wrote in *Horse and Hound*, 'the one really exceptional horse of the four was Be Fair.' Whether this is so is arguable, but being biased to this horse because he was mine, I am bound to agree. A highly intelligent, very compact and athletic chestnut, Be Fair was an exceptional person. He trod, step by step, the original fairy-tale life. He was five, proud and utterly singleminded when given to me by my parents for my fifteenth birthday. We grew up and learned together, moving along the proverbial ladder from the Pony Club through seven years to

Olympic Games. He managed to reach the heights despite me, surviving many more jockey errors born of inexperience than the three horses which followed him. Therein lies his exceptional quality.

His dream career is already honoured in his biography *Up, Up and Away*. Growing up only happens once. It is sufficient tribute to Be Fair that the profound relationship we shared could never be repeated.

There seems virtually nothing in common between Wide Awake, George and Killaire, except possibly that each of the three partnerships was triggered off by a telephone call . . .

Two

'You ought to come down and try this little horse, Lucinda. Sally, my daughter, has done a bit of this eventing lark on him – I think they were fourth at the Taunton Vale One-Day Event. Anyway, now Sally's getting married her mother doesn't want the horse to be wasted. He isn't very pretty, and he doesn't know much about the dressage game, but he's got a great "lep" in him, and he's as bold as they come out hunting.'

Bill Brake belongs to a famous West Country family of horse dealers. A superb natural horseman, I had come to know and respect him while hunting a borrowed young horse with the Blackmore Vale during the winter of 1972–3.

Bill's first wife, Mrs Vicki Phillips, had apparently noticed Be Fair and me on TV during our first Badminton the year before, in 1972. Bill no doubt said the right things when describing our hunting exploits together and encouraged Mrs Phillips in her idea to send me her horse to event.

Vicki Phillips was very attached to Wide Awake. However, she had always felt since buying him as a four-year-old through Jack Gittins that he had too much ability to remain solely in the hunting field. Mrs Phillips suggested, via Bill, that I come down to Somerset to try her horse.

In February 1973 I drove to Ilchester and rode a wiry, angular, bay seven-year-old. Bred by the Copes of Witney, he was out of their event mare, Serenade, by Hereward the Wake. He was barely 16.1 h.h., seemed tough, workman-like and far from beautiful. He could not have looked less like Be Fair who, in 1973, was my only gauge of a good event horse. Although smaller than Be Fair, he had a longer stride and felt ganglier and less balanced. We jumped only a few fences on Bill's farm as the horse had overreached out hunting a few days earlier and the cut had not healed properly. His power and boldness were not in question after those initial hedges, but the disdain he accorded this rider's wishes left doubt in her mind from the start as to her ability to ride him.

I was delighted and extremely flattered to be offered this opportunity. But first I had to return home and discuss with my father the financial problems of keeping someone else's horse.

I was just nineteen, earning no money and spending all my time looking after Be Fair, who was aiming for our second Badminton. Understandably Mrs Phillips was not prepared to pay for having her horse taken away from her and ridden by a little whippersnapper who had only been round Badminton and Burghley once. It was touch and go whether or not she would allow him to leave her at all. For some time my parents and I had worried that there was no horse on its way up the ladder behind Be Fair. Unsuccessfully we had tried to solve this problem. We had sold on the first young horse which we bought three years previously. He grew to 17.3 h.h. Like many, our family was handicapped by a tight budget. The next buy was my first solo attempt: a flashy chestnut with a white face and three white socks which moved beautifully, jumped as if it had no back end, which in truth it hardly did have, and stayed sound for intervals of a week at a time.

We could not miss this opportunity. Wide Awake seemed the ideal answer.

Within a week of his arrival at our home, Appleshaw, he was lame. The hunting overreach still seemed to be causing a problem. A fetlock might have twisted when he jumped into himself and maybe he had tweaked it again jumping at home.

A fortnight later he was sound and ready to start work

1a.
Be Fair managed to reach the heights despite me. Luhmühlen, 1975. (*Manfred Rakebrand, Bild Zeitung*)

1b. Be Fair aiming for his second Badminton, 1973. (*Clive Hiles*)

2a.
Guarding Be Fair,
the first Badminton
champion, Oliver Plum,
constant companion
and general nuisance.

2b.
Wide Awake,
recently arrived
at Appleshaw
in 1973.

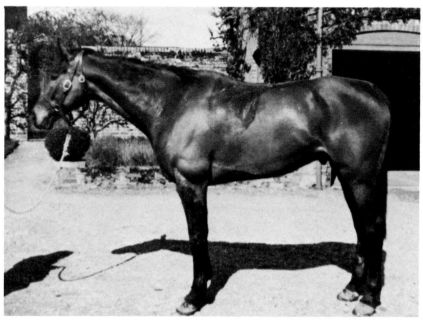

3a.
Uncertain of each other.
Our first novice event
at Coombe Bissett.
Wide Awake, 1973.

3b.
A better ride.
Wide Awake competing
at Tidworth, 1974.
(*John Elliot*)

4. Daddy with his charge, Be Fair,
winner of the Open Intermediate at Crookham.
(*Findlay Davidson*)

5a.
Wide Awake and Harley are
loaded into the plane,
bound for Boston to compete
in the Ledyard Three-Day
Event. June 1975.

5b. With no apparent justification,
Wide Awake suddenly kicked out at Harley. (*Warren Patriquin*)

6. Be Fair knew exactly who had become the new European Champion. Luhmühlen, 1975. (*Hugo Czerny*)

7a.
The last fence, and
the end of an inspired
cross-country round.
Wide Awake,
Badminton, 1976.
(*Desmond O'Neill*)

7b.
The victory lap –
'The thrill of
achievement only
surpassed by the
thrill of
communication.'
Wide Awake,
Badminton, 1976.
(*Leslie Lane*)

8a.
My 'hunter'.
Joanna checks
Killaire's girths.
Burghley, 1976.
(*Thomas Noel*)

8b.
Killaire over
the first part
of the Coffin,
Burghley, 1976.
(*John F. Hughes*)

again. At that time, Daddy had not decided that bars across stable doors were a compulsory safety measure. One minute Wide Awake's cheeky brown face with its sharp white star in the centre was looking innocently over his half door, the next, he was nipping across the lawn having undone his own bolt. He shot through the woodshed, up the garden steps, left-handed across the kitchen garden through the far gateway and dived down the back drive at a gallop.

He had been so quick in his escape that none of us had had a chance to head him off. Breathless and horrified, Mummy, Daddy and I stood at the top of the back drive watching helplessly. A van was coming down the road from the right, its speed and distance matching Wide Awake's as he thundered down the drive at right angles to the road. With an appalling and lifeless thud the inevitable happened. Wide Awake hit the front of the van, somersaulted, and was bounced off the bonnet high into the air, like a beach ball, landing twelve feet away on the other side of the road. He must have broken something – if he was still alive.

He struggled to his feet. He stood for a brief moment hanging his off-hind and then limped up the road in a worried, fast trot.

The two unfortunate and blameless men in the van were unharmed but needed a strong drink and a new bonnet. Unbelievably Wide Awake suffered only superficial scrapes and bruising and was lame for barely a week. Fear of traffic following that day was, I think, the only fear he knew in all his life.

During that April of 1973 he was still recovering, doing some slow road work, when Be Fair drew the first side of the square. To our complete disbelief he won Badminton, over what was generally assumed to be the toughest cross-country course seen there. Wide Awake sent Be Fair a telegram: 'Congratulations – me next year – love Wakey.'

I could not see any conceivable possibility of this happening – next year or any year. In our brief acquaintance so far Wide Awake and I were not amalgamating well. He was the opposite in nearly every way to Be Fair. Far from possessing a gentlemanly outlook, he proved to be the original pugnacious, cheeky schoolboy. He took the greatest delight in doing as much to annoy us as he could – mundane annoyances, such as backing someone into a corner of his stable; or waiting until the mucking-out dustbin was brim full and then backing into it and knocking it all over the clean floor. When a protective exercise boot was being put on a front leg, he would lift up his foot and wave it quietly around, refusing to put it down until he was certain of scoring a direct hit on a toe, or better still, a bended knee.

Riding him was the same story. The only type of horse that I had any idea how to ride was a naturally balanced, extremely cautious Be Fair, who always took the greatest care of himself and his rider. Suddenly I found myself astride a less-balanced, straggly seven-year-old who never looked twice at anything he was asked to jump. The trouble was that often he did not seem to look once either. To Wide Awake the bit was a waste of time. Like any other horse that I might have ridden he certainly did not accept the bit, quite possibly therefore it was my fault and not his, but his stringy, straight neck showed little sign that it knew how to bend or flex. Schooling was much the same sort of joke as it had been for two or three years with Be Fair. Cantering without changing legs behind on most turns was too difficult for both of us. Frustrations built up between me and this independent individual who was supposed to be next in line to the Badminton winner.

Probably the worst part involved in riding a horse for someone else is telephoning them to tell them bad news. Mrs Phillips was telephoned three times in the first eight weeks. When I had had to ring and tell her of Wide Awake's rendezvous with the car bonnet, she was remarkably calm. But the third bit of bad news was nearly too much for us both. This time Wakey had been laid off by Mr Mahon, our Lambourn vet, owing to a slightly strained check-ligament.

Consequently, that was that for the spring events. Entries were withdrawn and all hopes of novice eventing had to wait until July. Unfortunately, they had to wait two months longer and another dreaded telephone call had to be made.

Until 1973 there had been no need to have any help in the stables. Soon it began to seem a necessity to find a working pupil to help. The first girl did what everybody does once, until he or she learns the hard way: she picked out Wakey's front feet in the yard and then in preference to taking him into his stable, or tying him up, went round to the back and picked up his hind foot. Never slow to seize an opportunity this was too good a chance to miss and once again Wide Awake danced off across the lawn. By the time he reached the concreted open gateway to the yard he was moving at a fast canter. In his haste not to lose a second lest one of us catch him up, he whipped through the gateway on the turn. His feet slipped on the concrete and his hip bone ricocheted off the gate post. Uncharacteristically he stopped thirty yards later in front of a field fence and allowed himself to be caught. Hopping on one hind leg he was led back to his stable.

The vet presumed that he had chipped a piece of bone from his hip. In a few weeks' time he hoped it would settle and cause him no more trouble.

Eventually we did arrive at our first novice event – Coombe Bissett in mid-September, seven months after Wide Awake had first come to Appleshaw. He completed one more event, at Tweseldown, before going to the Wylye Novice Three-Day Event. He treated novice one-day event cross-country courses with scorn. He never seemed to notice the fences. If he was on the right stride he cleared them, if he was on the wrong one he hit them. The more arrangements I made in front of the fence in an attempt to warn him not to hit it, the more flippantly he would jump. I could not fathom it. Be Fair had always needed switching on well before each fence and quite often he required encouragement in the last few strides. This was the only way I knew how to ride, but evidently it was not the right way to ride Wide Awake. For a long time I felt that the hit-or-miss rides he gave me were my fault because I was perhaps not preparing him sufficiently before each fence. It was nearly two years before it began to dawn on me that maybe it was the preparation itself which was upsetting him and making him lose his concentration. It was a further year before I dared to sit still and do nothing on an approach.

He did prove a slightly easier ride across country in the Wylye Novice Three-Day Event. The roads and tracks and steeplechase phases, which occur in a three-day event but not in a one-day event, took the edge off him, and this left him a little more prepared to size up the oncoming fences using a modicum of his ample brain. He show-jumped more carefully too, and a double clear earned him fourth place.

Mike Tucker, Badminton competitor and always a great morale booster, was commentating during the Wylye Three-Day Event. He had admired Wakey's cross-country round. 'You've got another good horse there, you lucky girl,' he said. This I felt was high praise. For the first time I was pleased with Wakey too.

Our trust in each other barely existed before Wylye. Therefore we had much catching up to do in constructing the foundations of our mutual confidence. A week later Wakey suffered his only fall in competition, at the Taunton One-Day Event.

A novice three-day event does not appear to take much out of certain types of horses. It seemed a good idea, therefore, to do Taunton; maybe the usually over-exuberant child would be more prepared to concentrate. It was not a good idea at all. To my surprise Wakey fell at an early fence. He lay on the wet heavy ground, panting for a short while – possibly he had winded himself. I wanted to continue and jump a few more fences as I did not like to end a day – let alone a season – on such a bad note. The fence judge told me that I could not possibly continue: 'Don't you see your horse is tired out?' Tiredness was the last thing in the world that I expected Wakey to suffer. Obediently I led him back to his dejected owner and thence to a brief winter holiday at Appleshaw.

Six weeks' hunting in Leicestershire was Be Fair's promised treat for having survived the rigours of the European Championships in Kiev in September and a horrible fall. Normally I was too fearful of injury to hunt my experienced event horse. Kiev, I feared, may have taken the fun out of jumping for Be Fair, and some hunting might serve to re-inspire him. It proved necessary and it did the trick. Wide Awake had completed only three horse trials in one whole year. His experience was sorely lacking and so he went with Be Fair to Leicestershire to broaden his outlook.

During his hunting Wide Awake showed a trait which continues to puzzle me to this day.

The field which hunts with the Cottesmore numbers upwards of two hundred people. Invariably it means frequent queuing for fences and gateways. Accepting this enforced discipline for a while, suddenly Wakey could tolerate it no longer. If he was forced to queue for longer than ten or fifteen seconds, he froze. He would stand like a statue, refusing to move in any direction. In front of fences, on narrow footbridges and in gateways he turned to stone, thereby, and much to my embarrassment, blocking the way of many a side-saddled figure with veiled face, or pink-coated gentleman under elegant top hat. Once, he petrified about fifty yards from a boundary hedge. Within seconds of being pulled up to see which way hounds were turning, he froze. Over two hundred horses fanning to his left and right galloped past and jumped the hedge in front of him. Nothing could mobilise Wide Awake. When the last horse was out of sight his muscles untensed, his back dropped and he picked up where he left off as if nothing had happened. It *had* happened though for we lost the hunt and missed the run.

While attempting to avoid a similar game of statues I landed myself in Oakham hospital for three days and was not allowed to ride for six weeks.

Hounds had found and were setting off across the Leicestershire countryside in full cry. The usual fire of excitement and apprehension lit up the field. A myriad horses galloped for a corner in which there was a small narrow fence, the only negotiable exit to the field. Although near to the front Wakey would still have to wait his turn to jump. In my anxiety not to miss another run as I felt him begin to freeze, I kicked him at the hedge which lay to one side of the rails. It was no ordinary hedge, being as wide as it was tall. Five foot, I felt sure, would be within his immense scope. With only four strides of canter, and with horses popping over the rail on his left to take his attention, Wakey did not make it. He veered sharply left as he took off and cannoned into the back end of someone jumping the rails. More than that I do not remember until waking up in the car of my rescuer, Mr Boone.

The infuriated remarks that must have reverberated through the field as I lay for dead directly in the path of the field's only exit, have thankfully only to be imagined: 'Arrogant Badminton winners – think they know it all.'

Wakey did not have any more hunting. Two weeks later Mrs Phillips had hoped to have a day on him. He started to cough shortly before and his unfortunate owner was disappointed once again.

In November 1973, at exactly the time I was chewing my sheets in Oakham hospital, a fluffy-coated, hairy-heeled, bay five-year-old was arriving from Northern Ireland at his new home in Sussex.

'I thought I sent you to buy me a Badminton winner not a

. . . cart-horse. What in heaven's name have you spent my money on?' The owner was new to horse trials and had wanted to buy a top-class horse. His prospective rider, equally inexperienced, had been sent to Ireland in response to a flashy advertisement describing a 16.3 h.h. event horse called Killaire . . .

Three

1974 began in much the same way as 1973 had ended. In mid-March a fall on the flat in my fourth and last point-to-point at Larkhill put paid to my collar bone and the first three weeks of the event season. It was imperative that Wide Awake, already eight years old, should miss no further opportunities to gain experience.

Bruce Davidson, the celebrated American event rider, had come to England to ride at Badminton. Bruce, with his wife and their two horses, was based at Wylye where the Russells have built up one of the world's best-equipped horse trials training centres. Bruce had praised Wakey highly when he had seen him during a cross-country practice at Wylye earlier in the spring. 'He's just like a smaller edition of Plain Sailing,' he enthused; 'he has the same extra wedge of muscle where his bottom joins the top back end of his second thigh. I sure bet he's a power house.' Plain Sailing was a fine and rare specimen of a class, quality English Hunter. In 1966 he was sold to America by Posie Kopanski and during the following eight years he represented the USA with various jockeys in every international three-day event team.

Bruce therefore was delighted to have the opportunity of training Wide Awake for a month and riding him in his first intermediate horse trials.

Wakey's legs had been none too clean and hard since the day he arrived with his overreach. We always had to keep an eye on them and frequently a cooling hose or leg lotion was needed to prevent them filling.

Three days after Wakey had been deposited at Wylye a

worried Bruce telephoned: 'I'm real scared of Wide Awake's off-foreleg. It's coming up all warm and beginning to fill and he only had a light work-out yesterday. I'm frightened that if I do any more work with him I'll break him down. I guess you had better take him home. I'm real sorry to bring such bad news.' Bad news indeed it was, but with Wide Awake around we were becoming accustomed to it. Once again it was a very different story from that of Be Fair who in all seven years of our competing together had us on tenterhooks only once.

We had had Wakey just thirteen months and to date we had experienced five nasty surprises. This, the fifth, sounded like the final one. Obviously he was about to break down. In direct contrast to the rest of him, his legs must be 'soft'.

In order to lessen the ultimate blow we decided to ask his owner Vicki Phillips and Mr Mahon, the vet, to meet Wakey, Bruce and ourselves at Wylye the following day. We would all hear his fate diagnosed first-hand and a further telephone call of doom could thus be avoided.

Sombre-faced we stood waiting as Mr Mahon bent down on his knees to examine Wide Awake's legs. I felt sure he would advise, 'Fire his legs and rest him for a year.'

Eventually, straightening up from beside Wide Awake's front legs, he dusted his hands and looked at us through his glasses. Unsmiling he looked back at Wakey's forelegs. The other front leg had become hot and had started to swell too. He was breaking down on *both* front legs.

'What have you put on these legs?' he questioned Bruce.

'Some special cooling lotion I use on all my horses. I put it on the first evening he arrived as his legs didn't handle that clean even then.'

'Well,' stated the vet with no hint of rebuke, 'these legs have been blistered.'

His skin was not normally sensitive but, true to his luckless form, it had managed to be allergic to Bruce's scrupulously applied cooling lotion. Within another day he had two bed posts for front legs. He spent the following three weeks resting and being fed with Epsom salts in an attempt to take the heat out of his legs.

During that time I rode like an imbecile around Badminton on the hot favourite, Be Fair. A straightforward course had been built to paste over memories of the previous year. There was only one difficult and complex fence on the course. Over this I determined to go the most direct and impressive way. Be Fair, I felt, had to pay for exploding in his dressage test. During one crashing somersault at the 'S' fence I learned two very important lessons. Firstly, not to take it out on my horse on the cross-country solely because of my own inability to sort out the dressage. Secondly, to adhere to my father's wisdom: 'You are out on that course to jump clean around it – not to impress the TV and thrill the crowds.'

Wide Awake's legs recovered to a reasonable size in time to do his one and only intermediate before the Tidworth Three-Day Event in mid-May.

We were still at loggerheads. I fought him in an attempt to make him jump more carefully; he disliked interference and fought back. Even before Tidworth, his owner Vicki knew we were not happy together and tactfully suggested that if I thought we were at odds maybe I ought to send him back to her. Now that her daughter Sally had settled down with her husband in Cornwall, she suggested Wakey was sent down to her. Vicki quoted the case of a famous jockey who had found that he could not click with a certain racehorse, in order to make me feel that it was no disgrace to be unable to acclimatise to Wide Awake.

It did feel a disgrace though. I was convinced of Wide Awake's outstanding abilities just as I was convinced that if I could not learn to ride him I would never advance my principal ambition. I knew Be Fair was exceptional and that my attitude and manner of riding, purely by chance, fitted him like a Savile Row suit. Equally I knew that he was the only horse I understood how to ride. The ambition to be able one day to step on any horse and feel how to ride him to the best of his ability, has always held greater significance for me than that of recording great triumphs.

Although I could not love him as yet, I did not want to part with him. Vicki generously allowed him to stay on at Appleshaw.

With much help and patience from David Hunt our dressage became slightly more presentable. Wakey now kept his hind legs united at canter and looked as if he was on the bit most of the time. His evasion was that he tended to lose impulsion, drop behind the bit and over-bend – once again the reverse of Be Fair who bubbled away above the bit. Wakey lay fourth after the dressage, the first phase of the Tidworth Three-Day Event.

He seemed remarkably fit after his three weeks' lay-off considering he had been working for less than a month. Bruce had mapped out a programme of fitness for Wakey, pursuing a weird method called interval training. He told me that I had more chance of having him fit in time, without his suspect legs giving him trouble, if I adopted this system. The idea of interval training had been brought from France to the USA by Jack Le Goff, when he arrived in America in 1971 to coach their three-day event team.

After three years' experience Bruce strongly believed in the method's ability to render a horse fit with less strain on his legs. (See Appendix 1.)

Wide Awake's fitness was in no doubt on cross-country day at Tidworth. He proved very difficult to hold still and allow himself to be washed down in the 'Box', the roped-off enclosure used for the ten-minute compulsory halt before the cross-country. He did not appear to have noticed the exertions involved in completing phases A, B and C – approximately nine miles' trotting and cantering down roads and tracks, interrupted by a two-mile gallop around a steeplechase course. He buffed and bored my non-horsy elder sister Karol, who was bravely trying to hold him still. He whizzed in tiny circles around Joanna, Be Fair's first full-time nanny, who was trying to wash him down. He trod on Daddy who was vainly attempting to employ a sweat-scraper. It seemed that he must have remembered from Wylye that the most exciting bit, the cross-country, was yet to come. Somehow he was held still long enough to put the saddle back on him, and me onto the saddle, before we were mercifully flagged away on the four-mile cross-country. Ten minutes later we returned, intact and without penalties. Wakey had given me a slightly safer ride than I expected. He was thinking a little more and hitting a little less and managed the difficult fences better than the easy ones. Generally he hit any fence off a turn, and sometimes very hard. For reasons that Wakey kept secret, if I interfered with him just in front of a fence, such as guiding him round a corner or checking him in front of a combination of fences, he would hollow against my hands and jump flat and carelessly. It was very much later that I learned to use my legs in preference to my hands to turn him.

To our amazement Wakey ended the cross-country day in the lead of his section. With a very disjointed fifteen months' acquaintanceship and only three novice events and one intermediate behind us, it was a welcome break in our mutual fortunes.

The rejoicing lasted barely twenty-four hours because there was still no true understanding between us. The following day, through more flat and careless jumping, three show-jumps crashed onto the hard-baked chalk ground. In similar fashion we descended from first to fourth. Poor Vicki – more disappointment. But worse was to come.

After Tidworth Wakey's near-fore was showing definite signs of wear. Following Daddy's theory that prevention was always better than cure, we asked Nipper Constance if he would look at the leg. Nipper is an extremely experienced and able surgeon and since giving up regular practice a few years previously had concentrated principally on tendon surgery. His advice was to 'tendon split' both legs and lay Wide Awake off for the remainder of the year. He thought firing was barbaric and was determined that surgery would prove equally effective and infinitely more civilised for the patient. His advice was readily taken, particularly as Vicki kindly agreed to finance the operation.

Meanwhile I drove to Warendorf in Germany to spend two weeks studying under the German show-jumping ace Hans Günther Winkler who has won more gold medals than he owns fingers on one hand. We were all growing a little bored with my lack of expertise in the show-jumping phase. It was becoming increasingly evident that only Be Fair was prepared to make amends for my misdemeanours. Future horses might not; Wide Awake did not.

Winkler found it evident too. The third day I was at Warendorf he asked me, 'What did they say you have done? Did they say you have won Badminton? What sort of horse is this then, this Be Fair, if he can win Badminton in spite of you?'

Two of the most valuable weeks in my education ensued. I had always known my limitations and realised that any success Be Fair and I had had was due to his unique ability and the firm partnership we had formed together.

Hans Winkler was the only person actually prepared to tell me what I, and no doubt others, already knew.

'You are not a natural artist.' At the same time he told me what no one else had ever told me, 'Riding is an art that *can* be taught – I had to learn.'

I did not return home a well-polished show-jumper and still, unfortunately, have not grasped the technique as I would like to. During those two weeks, through riding a series of different horses for the first time, and being under the constant surveillance of a man who was as skilful a teacher as he is a rider, I began to see a crack of light in the dark shroud enclosing the mysteries of the art of riding. I did not find much more light until I returned three years later to Germany's top dressage centre. A slightly wider chink appeared after a month's stay there.

There have been several occasions since that fortnight in 1974 when, through a tantalising lack of feel and comprehension, I have nearly sunk without trace. Winkler's conviction and self-proof that it is possible to learn the art and that it does not necessarily have to be a natural gift, has kept me afloat.

For all the struggles behind and all the toil that still lies ahead, I am indebted to Hans Winkler for those words. I believe that I am lucky not to be a 'natural'. Often I wonder if that small band of Nature's geniuses can actually appreciate the pleasure of displaying their art well when they have never known what it feels like to do it badly.

Shortly after returning from Germany in June, I drove to a farm near Badminton to see Wide Awake convalescing after his operation. Despite the fact that he had propelled his head straight through a glass window the first evening he arrived there, Nipper Constance liked Wide Awake.

Twice during the ensuing weeks Nipper had mused, 'He'll win Badminton one day that little horse, you know.' I was encouraged by his enthusiasm although I was quite sure that no other horse, least of all Wide Awake, would be cooperative enough to win Badminton for me. Returning from a visit to Wakey I crept into Badminton Park. Under the late afternoon sun I sat cross-legged in the long summer grass surrounding the Normandy Bank, relishing the chance to be in these special surroundings entirely alone. I wondered what had made Nipper so convinced of Wide Awake's future.

Four

Adhering to a streak of madness which possibly emanates from my father's Irish ancestry I decided to try and ride three horses at Badminton in 1975. Be Fair was plenty experienced, but the other two most definitely were not.

Ellie May was a broad-beamed chestnut lady with white spots, four high white stockings and a white face. Her past was interesting. She started life as a show-jumper in David Broome's yard. She was then bought by Captain Naylor-Leyland and evented by his son at novice and intermediate level for two years. She was the first horse that I had ever been offered as a 'chance' ride, and excitedly I partnered her in two advanced events at the end of the autumn of 1974. She completed clear rounds across country in both these and she had won one novice three-day event when ridden by Pammy Sivewright in 1973. Ostensibly she was qualified for Badminton.

Wide Awake was already a nine-year-old but his credentials comprised only a novice three-day event, an intermediate one-day event and an intermediate three-day event, liberally sprinkled with varying lengths of time in convalescence. In 1975 this represented sufficient qualification for Badminton.

Judy Mackie, Daddy's part-time secretary, started Wide Awake on a month's walking exercise in November while I tried to help some charming Greeks with their riding in Athens. Wakey was bound to be a handful after six months off and would need someone with more experience and strength than Joanna. Judy was ideal. Joanna, though extremely plucky, was picked off her tiny feet at Wide

Awake's will and swung through the air on the end of his headcollar rope. Oblivious to any intentions other than his own, he soon found that he was never taken out of his stable, not even to be turned out in the field, unless he wore a bridle.

Preparing three horses for Badminton during that winter was hard work for Jo, our working pupil Emma, and myself. Along with three Badminton prospects were two youngsters, and Hysterical, Be Fair's dotty thoroughbred girlfriend who belonged to her breeder, dear Mrs Ivory. Sadly, both Mrs Ivory and Hysterical have since passed into the next world. Hysterical was with me for four years during which time I failed miserably to un-dotty her and eventually she returned home to have babies.

In mid-March Be Fair accidentally hurt someone for the first time in his life. Emma was riding up the road towards the gallops owned by Toby Balding, a local and extremely generous racehorse trainer, in order to meet me and exchange Be Fair for Wide Awake when the latter had finished his work-out. Be Fair shied and slipped over on the road, catching Emma's ankle between the tarmac and the stirrup. Despite great pain she was sure that she had not broken it and bravely continued. Alas, for the next six weeks she was hopping around with a fertiliser bag over her plaster determined not to back out of our triplicate attack.

The challenge presented by producing three horses sound and fit to compete at Badminton was as formidable as that involved in actually trying to ride all three around Badminton. So much can go wrong in the build-up. Wide Awake for one nearly did not make it.

He and I were having a cross-country school on the Wylye downs under Lady Hugh Russell's expert supervision. We were supposed to bounce in and out of a 'V' fence near its apex. I gave Wide Awake the impossible task of bouncing in and out of a two-yard space between the rails instead of a five-yard one further down. I had mistaken my line of approach. Somehow, and with an excess of ingenuity, he negotiated the obstacle without appearing to harm himself as he slid over the second part hitting it with his forearm. He did not fall but I fell off. I was furious with myself and wondered how I could possibly make such a wretched and stupid error. Why should any horse jump for me again if I did things like that?

That was too much for Sheila Willcox, who had owned Be Fair's father Fair and Square. She happened to be spending that afternoon at Wylye watching the schooling session.

Sheila had won Badminton three times. I respected her enormously and I owe her much gratitude for what she said to me later that afternoon.

She felt that I had won Badminton too early, before fully appreciating the intricacies and difficulties of three-day eventing. Be Fair was a brilliant horse, she said, and he should never have lost a competition in the last two years. The message was clear: if I wished to prove that Be Fair's Badminton win two years before had been no fluke, I would have to start taking a great deal more trouble. Sheila, like Lady Hugh Russell, emphasised the importance of learning accuracy in riding across country.

'If you decide to jump a fence over a specific point, you must learn enough self-discipline to ensure that your horse does jump it at exactly that point. You will never reach the top if you cannot achieve this.'

It was after this incident at Wylye that Wide Awake began to pull out stiff in one shoulder every morning. It was not severe and would work off in a few minutes. Despite rest later in the year he never again ran up sound first thing in the morning.

A short time later, while misbehaving, Wide Awake backed into a tree and bruised a hind leg. Every day he was boxed up and driven five miles to the nearest river where, piled high with rugs to shield him from biting March winds, he stood in the cold water in the hopes that it would alleviate the bruising. Instead of emptying, his leg filled more each day and became increasingly hot and painful. I thought there must be something seriously wrong with his hind joint and Badminton began to look dubious.

Eventually we discovered that he had developed a mud fever infection through a small graze on the back of his leg. There is one sure way to aggravate mud fever – and that is to wet it.

The three Badminton prospects started the season in a positive manner. Be Fair won the open intermediate at Crookham, Wide Awake was third in the intermediate and Ellie May was sixth.

Ten days later in the pouring rain Be Fair, Wide Awake, Jo and I went to the Downlands Horse Trials in the 'ice cream van', our little Lambourn Caravella two-horsebox. I could not attract Wide Awake's attention in his dressage. He was not liable to blow up like Be Fair – he used more subtle evasions. When the day's dressage was completed I took him back into the same arena and worked him. No progress was registered and we returned to the horsebox no longer on speaking terms with each other. I was particularly upset by this and quite possibly Wide Awake was in a similar, if better disguised, state of mind. I was in the horsebox putting on his roller, standing between him and the central dividing bar between the two stalls. Maybe it was bottled fury at our misunderstanding over the dressage which made him display another extraordinary trait. Quietly and determinedly he bent his head and neck away from me and pushed his rib cage onto mine. Slowly he began to squash me against the dividing bar. This sort of thing had happened before with other horses and a shout and a kick normally stopped the game. But Wide Awake leaned in deadly earnest. He continued quietly to press what felt like his entire fifteen-hundred-pound bodyweight against my stomach. As my liver began to concertina into my vertebrae I panicked, realising he was not going to abandon this new idea. There was nothing to do but scream for help. With what little breath there remained in me, I yelled like I had never been forced to yell before. Not a second too soon the passenger door flew open and in popped a few unknown anxious faces. Rapidly digesting the situation they leapt into the box and pulled Wakey forward as they pushed him sideways – thus releasing a new Twiggy from the bar. I was dearly thankful that it was a bar and not the partition that used to divide the box. Wide Awake had decided that he could not spread his legs sufficiently wide with a partition and its presence had made him scrabble and slip, like a learner skater, on every corner.

That incident scared me. I had always suspected Wakey of having a devious, albeit good-humoured nature which he would use to antagonise humans rather than to help them. But this retaliation, I felt, was a sign of his genuine dislike for me. It made me think long and hard about him and his complex character. He was extremely independent, but unlike Be Fair he did not know how to refuse a jump. He would never give up. Essentially he was a winner. I believe he had become accustomed to being king-pin in the eyes of Sally and Vicki, both of whom had adored him and looked after him for three years. Like so many horses he was incredibly sensitive to atmosphere. When he arrived at Appleshaw he must have run headlong into the regal wall, the kingly aura, which surrounded the one and only. Be Fair's strong and bewitching personality absorbed nearly all my love and understanding. There was little enough to spare for those who did not conform to his example. The two horses were never friends. They could not be turned out in the same field together because they fought. Often I wonder that if I had never known Be Fair would it still have taken me nearly three years before Wide Awake and I began to understand one another?

Pat Burgess, who has played a vital part in helping me with my jumping since Pony Club days with Be Fair, was worried that I wished to run Wide Awake at Badminton so early in his career.

'Why do you want to take him this year? He's got so much ability but he's had no chance to gain much experience. The two of you just don't quite fit together yet. So why are you so determined to go?'

The reasons were three-fold and none of them was particularly well founded. Firstly, I had set myself the challenge of trying to train and ride three horses at Badminton. Now that the rare opportunity had presented itself I was not going to be easily dissuaded. Secondly, his owner wanted him to go to Badminton. Having hunted and hunter-trialled him herself for three years she felt his talent and ability were so remarkable that he could have done it the first year he came to me. The final reason that served at the time to justify the first two was a case of 'kill or cure'. Either the huge fences at Badminton would dispel his nonchalance and illuminate his latent brilliance, or they would not. I did not understand how else to teach him to respect his fences and to jump cleanly and safely like my cat-like Be Fair.

What a dangerous attitude. Very occasionally it may work but the odds are heavily against it. Since then I have witnessed one or two horses of great potential ruined when faced with a big course before they have gained sufficient experience to handle the problems confidently. Through boldness they may negotiate the course reasonably success-fully but in so doing they probably frighten themselves. Consequently they may never become the star horses they were destined to be.

There is a point in every good horse's life when a trip round Badminton will construct, rather than destroy, the foundations of a glowing future. Taking the horse before this point has been reached is akin to kicking away the guy ropes of a tent. The tent may still stand but it needs only a light shake to bring it down.

A mainsail must be carefully and thoroughly rigged in order to withstand a storm. So too must an event horse be prepared in order to survive, with confidence intact, the worst and most undermining circumstances.

It is not in jest that I say I am looked after. Somebody up there must be keeping a thorough watch on my antics. Badminton was water-logged. All fifty-five competitors sloshed through their dressage. No sooner had Wide Awake, the last to go, unstuck his feet from the arena, than the loud speakers spluttered into life and declared Badminton 1975 cancelled.

At the time the disappointment for everyone was immense, and especially for the loyal band of friends who had teamed together to help in our mammoth task of running three horses at Badminton. Our willing helpers even included Nanny, who had come from her home near Folkestone especially to try to maintain me in sparkling boots and clean breeches for each of the three horses.

Be Fair had finally rewarded David Hunt's patience and understanding while educating us over the past five years. He had produced one of his very few genuinely fine tests which left him in the lead after the dressage. Wide Awake lay seventh and Ellie May was a surprisingly good twelfth. In retrospect I reckon that that was probably where the success story would have ended. Be Fair could barely jump when the going was as deep as it was that year. Ellie May proceeded to the Punchestown Three-Day Event the following month and fell twice on a much easier cross-country course. And I have yet to see a combination as out of touch as Wide Awake and me complete Badminton satisfactorily.

The cancellation was a merciful escape, not only from the consequences of my misguided challenge, but also from a very awkward situation which had brewed during that last afternoon of dressage. One of the judges had blinked twice in the morning when he opened his programme and realised he was to be judging me twice that day. He had already judged me once the day before. He summoned the organisation in the form of Colonel Frank Weldon and said that he refused to judge me unless I declared one of my three horses Hors Concours. The FEI (Fédération Équestre Internationale) rules had changed since anyone in England had last looked at them. It was now forbidden for one rider to ride more than two horses in a three-day event. Eventually, it was decreed that I did not even have a choice. The last horse would automatically be nominated as the one to run Hors Concours. It would have to happen to poor Vicki. The last horse was Wide Awake. Understandably she was upset. She wanted her horse to run but saw no point in him floundering through the mud across those huge fences in terrible ground, just for the exercise. There was only one conceivable hope of escape from that particular problem, and it was granted.

A bay seven-year-old had already dashed his owner's Badminton hopes the year before, in 1974. On that occasion the British Horse Society had informed the owner that he was unable to enter his six-year-old horse and its rider as neither had competed in a three-day event and therefore neither was qualified to enter. Killaire was saved yet again from a trip round Badminton before he was ready, only this time, in 1975, it was by the rain.

Five

A shimmering hot day in mid-June saw Wide Awake tow Joanna across the tarmac of Heathrow Airport. He was bored with waiting and bored with plane-spotting. He marched Joanna determinedly towards Sue Hatherly's Harley, who was patiently awaiting his turn to be loaded, and cannoned into his flank – just for fun.

Six exceptionally lucky horses and riders were flying to Boston, USA, on a trip, with all expenses paid by our hosts, to compete against them in the Ledyard Three-Day Event.

The day after we arrived in the USA the six British riders were asked to line up on their horses for a press photograph. Wide Awake stood on the outside of the line, next to the Ledyard 1973 title-holders Harley and Sue Hatherly. Standing stock still one minute, Wide Awake suddenly moved sideways the next, and with no apparent justification kicked at Harley. He had never kicked anything before and it appeared to be an uncanny predetermined attempt to eradicate the opposition. Luckily it failed, and Harley was left unscathed if offended.

Ledyard was to be my own personal testing ground. My self-confidence had gradually flaked away over the past year and a half. Eventually only the raw truth remained to face me. I was twenty-one and I was no good at three-day eventing. I was doing stupid things, such as wrecking Wide Awake's cross-country practice at Wylye, and losing my way with Be Fair on the steeplechase phase and fourth place with it in the 1974 World Championships. More indicative than this, however, was the fact that good horses were continually falling with me. In the last five major three-day events I had incurred five falls.

Before leaving England I told my sister, Karol, that if I could not stay upright with Wide Awake at Ledyard I would feel bound to give up eventing. It did not seem fair that good horses should continue to be burdened with my presence and my errors.

Wide Awake first found a place in my heart on that boiling-hot afternoon of the cross-country day at Ledyard. It was not an easy course and he went clear. Possibly this was partly due to the sunstroke which hit me and left me feeling sufficiently sick and weak not to interfere much with his cross-country. It also enabled him to bolt on the steeplechase. Whatever the reason it did not really matter. The result was the same. I no longer felt I should give up riding in horse trials. For the first time in our association Wakey produced a trump card exactly on cue.

However, his leniency to me on the cross-country was quickly counteracted in the show-jumping arena the next day. With familiar careless, flat jumping two poles fell. His owner had come all the way to the USA to see her horse relegated from fourth to eighth place. Although harassed by my inability to improve our show-jumping together, I left America with a small handful of confidence. A thin life-line had finally traversed the gulf between Wide Awake and me. Something had taken root that might, in time, germinate into a partnership. Mummy, Daddy and I were never in any doubt about Wide Awake's abilities. We only held doubts about my own ability to find the appropriate key to expose his talent.

Two months later in September, Be Fair crowned himself European Champion in Luhmühlen, West Germany. On his return he was greeted by Wide Awake, who meanwhile had been lodging with Mary Gordon-Watson. He was adorned with a Union Jack hanging from his neck in honour of Be Fair. Things were looking up. Confidence began to swell and with it came a little more feeling and understanding in my riding. This, coupled with the experience gained at Ledyard, produced an improving relationship between Wide Awake and me by the time we arrived in Boekelo, for the Dutch Three-Day Event in late October.

With a new trick always up his sleeve, Wide Awake unexpectedly decided to amuse himself in the dressage phase. Normally lazy and somewhat bored by dressage, in Boekelo the geranium pots decorating the arena suddenly became *objets d'horreurs*. At the slightest provocation he would have pounced on one. I sat like a mouse not daring to move lest he should, and between us we hoodwinked ourselves into an undeserving fifth place after the first phase.

That evening he discovered how to eat straw from his bed despite being muzzled in order that he should eat none, thereby keeping his wind clear for the following day's cross-country. He dug his bed up into a loose high pile and then plunged his head into the depths of the pile, disappearing up to the eyes. He re-emerged, ears pricked in triumph, as he munched a few stalks of straw that had fallen over the edge and into the bottom of the wire-mesh muzzle.

The speed and endurance test the following day became a speed, endurance and navigation test. The fog was so thick early in the day that the competitors were held up before the cross-country in order to allow it time to clear. The delay between ending phase C and starting the cross-country inevitably continued throughout the day. Wide Awake, running near the end, was most surprised. Instead of the usual ten-minute break after the roads and tracks he was led back to his stable for half an hour's rest. By the time he started the cross-country it was tea-time, and the fog had begun to close in again, denser every minute.

After half an hour with his feet up Wide Awake set off on the cross-country with more zeal than was safe, as he demonstrated at the second fence. Neither of us could see the first fence from the start, nor the second fence from the first. Luckily Boekelo is not a windy course and with three course walks beforehand it was possible to arrive in more or less the right place to find the next fence. There was sufficient time for the horse to size up the fence between first sighting it and jumping it and I do not think that lack of visibility was the reason for Wide Awake's onslaught at the second one. A rail had to be jumped onto a bank, off which we were to spring over a yawning ditch. Disregarding requests to approach slowly Wide Awake loosed himself into the air in front of the rail entertaining no thoughts whatsoever of touching down on the bank. Sticking both feet forward and leaning well back for safety I allowed the reins to slip through my hands as he stretched out his head and neck, further and further in his efforts to make the far side of the wide ditch. I was sure that the moment had finally arrived when his heedless nature was going to land us in big trouble. I had underestimated him. To help him he had a great angle in his shoulders and these he used as shock absorbers. With no more than a gentle curtsy as he landed on the far side of the ditch, thirty feet from where he took off, he galloped on into the fog. He jumped with more thought for the next few fences until he came to a combination off a turn in the woods. A parallel was followed a stride later by a stream. At the top of the far bank stood a small upright rail. It was imperative to approach slowly. Decelerating early, before he turned and could see the fence, was a waste of effort. Four strides away Wakey attacked. A massive leap over the parallel brought him to the stream's edge. He took off immediately again, and landed in a heap on the far bank breasting the rail. One front leg had to go somewhere as he was off balance; it went over the rail. Miraculously he kept enough balance to escape falling while the other three legs followed in a series of individual jerks and crashes.

1968 Olympic gold and silver medallist Major Derek Allhusen, who has been a wonderful adviser on many occasions, was watching this fence. He gave me a rocket afterwards for purposely accelerating into a fence that I should have been approaching slowly.

Notwithstanding those two uncomfortable moments and one other, this was the first time that Wide Awake had handled a cross-country course like a top-class horse. He jumped most of what was the biggest course seen in Boekelo using his body and his mind. With the unplanned risks he took, he was three-quarters of a minute faster than any of his rivals and started the show-jumping day with one fence in hand over the German Rudiger Schwarz.

We had been to Pat Burgess many times and to several shows during the summer to try to solve our show-jumping problems. We had worked out with Pat that the bitless bridle, which Wide Awake wore in Ledyard, was no help. I realised I must learn how to make my hands acceptable to him, and not simply evade the problem by taking the bit out of his mouth altogether. He used to come up against the contact I had with his mouth and hollow his back, thereby leaving his hocks well out behind him in the last few strides before a fence.

Things had improved somewhat by Boekelo but with the added tension electrifying the reins a clear round could never have been achieved without John Smart. John, an eventer and show-jumper himself, was there as a spectator, but was most willing to help anyone who wanted it. He stopped me riding with my hands and trying to shorten and place Wide Awake to make him round his back. Instead he made me sit still and allow Wakey the freedom to sort each fence out for himself. To my astonishment Wide Awake started to drop his head as he took off and round his back thereby being able to tuck up his legs. It was probably during that afternoon that I finally stumbled on the key to the technique Wide Awake required. He made sure that 1975 was glued in my memory forever as he capped an extraordinary year, which mixed the depths of depression with the heights of ecstasy, by winning the Dutch Championships.

He behaved impossibly in the prize-giving. Normally of a calm nature, albeit cantankerous, he appeared genuinely upset and over-excited, and very nearly lost control of himself. He began by standing calmly in front of the judges' box for a few minutes and then, in a fit of apparent madness and in excessively speedy reverse, he ended up behind the back line of his fellow competitors. He was evidently not accustomed to winning.

What a wonderful change to be able to telephone Vicki from Holland with *good* news.

Six

Boekelo brought out and confirmed the very best side of Wide Awake's character. His personality was transformed – schoolboy pranks were replaced by man-of-the-world wisdom.

Such a dramatic metamorphosis in a horse, in the space of one weekend, convinced me more than ever that horses must possess an extra sense. They are, I believe, hypersensitive to atmosphere in a way that we humans are not. And none more so than Wide Awake, as he portrayed through his extraordinary reaction to atmosphere when he was hunting, when he squashed me in the horsebox after our row in the dressage, and during the prize-giving in Boekelo.

A horse can have no idea that a ribbon hanging from his bridle indicates that he has done well. I believe that he appears to know when he has won because he is surrounded by an air of contentment from the humans about him, particularly in his home.

Wide Awake changed almost overnight because I believe he sensed that at last he was no longer surrounded by antagonism. He had made his own name, forged his own path, and he was genuinely loved and respected for it. No longer did he live in Be Fair's shadow.

I was not due to return from Iran, where I was spending three months failing to teach Persians to ride, until mid-January 1976. Judy, once again, had kindly agreed to step in and start Wide Awake's walking exercise. She was not needed. Feeling that Wide Awake had become so biddable since Holland, Joanna thought that she could manage to bring him up after Christmas and give him two weeks' walking on the roads for two hours a day. She had no problem.

Despite the change in him, Wide Awake was never able to lay aside his accident-prone tendencies. I had been at home from Iran only for a week before he went lame behind. During his daily half-hour's relaxation in the field, Joanna had seen him chasing my poor twenty-year-old pony, Jupiter. Apparently he had slipped up dashing down a bank and tweaked a muscle which put him out of action for a few days. This time, at least no competitions were forfeited. Be Fair was heading for the Olympic Games in Montreal in July and was consequently excused a visit to Badminton. Wide Awake and I worked at our jumping, mostly with Pat in her rented field full of tin cans and poles and a small set of show-jumps. We continued to build on the partnership that had begun to emerge at Boekelo. Earlier in that spring of 1976 I became obsessed with throwing the reins away and sitting up his neck; I felt he was less likely to hollow under me and hit fences if he had no weight on his back and no hands pulling at his mouth. To prove her point that this was not the way to deal with his hollowing, Pat erected two jumps on oil drums at right angles to one another. Jumping them first in my fashion and then by sitting down on his back and keeping a quiet, even contact, showed me that although I had to be sensitive and tactful I must remain sitting down in the saddle. I could not keep his hocks under him if my weight and balance were half way up his mane. Without his hocks he jumped recklessly.

In 1976 Wide Awake felt ready to take on the challenge of Badminton. Instead of simply promising it, he was beginning to show that he could operate like a really good horse. Badminton need not be pandered to – it could be attacked. That, I believe, is the best way to approach this great event. It is too big and too difficult to use as a school.

During the winter a small, sharp, dark-brown thorough-bred called Village Gossip, belonging to the Brookeboroughs in Northern Ireland, was bought for me by a generous benefactor, David Kingsley. Ridden by Katie O'Hara, Gossip had completed Burghley very impressively the previous autumn. I felt unjustified in having a third advanced horse procured for me and asked my mother if she felt it was necessary that we were so greedy.

'Be Fair is thirteen, we cannot expect him to go on for much longer. Wide Awake, well, he is only ten but his legs haven't been that good and how much more strain will they stand up to in the future and then who is there but the four-year-old?' She is a fair-minded, uncompetitive person, but she was strangely adamant that it was right to have Village Gossip. Maybe she had caught a glimpse of the future.

Wide Awake and Be Fair each did one one-day event that spring, at Brigstock. Both went very well, clear in show-jumping and cross-country and both had an identical time. Be Fair won his section, and Wide Awake, facing hotter competition, finished fifth in the other.

Ten days before Badminton Wide Awake was entered in a Grade B and C show-jumping class at Amberley Horse Show. I have never dared enter it since. It was huge and although beautifully built, it was certainly the biggest course that I had ever tried to jump. Wide Awake jumped it with consummate ease solely because I sat still, riveted to the saddle in fear of the towering fences.

Four and a half miles of cross-country course and more than forty-five fixed obstacles needs much familiarizing and studying of the problems involved. On the first of three walks around the Badminton cross-country course in 1976, I had not reached fences six and seven – the first Luckington Lane Crossing – before a surge of extra happiness rushed through me. Badminton is a very special place and I am always happy to be there. This extra surge was recognis-able, however, as similar to that which had filled me at moments walking the course before Be Fair had won Badminton in 1973. I possessed an unaccustomed feeling that Wide Awake could win. Whether he would or not, of course, was quite another matter, but this was the first time that I had had enough confidence in him for the possibility even to flash through my mind.

Confidence, harmony, partnership – call it what you like – is an interesting phenomenon. It is difficult to pin-point its ingredients but it is easy to recognise when its presence is lacking.

Cautious optimism was further encouraged by Wide Awake coincidentally being allotted the same stable that had been given to Be Fair in 1973. He had been ten years old then and Wakey was ten years old now.

His number, too, bore some hint of superstitious encouragement. It was 86. Provided the number holds some denomination of seven, it is usually lucky for me. After much thought, I decided 86 passed. 8 + 6 makes 14, and 2 × 7 makes 14. Far fetched but possible. Be Fair had been fifth with Number 43 and had won with Number 61. Try as I would, nothing could be made of Number 54, the number worn in 1974 when we fell at the 'S' fence.

The magic of Badminton: inspiration exudes from every one of its immortal oak and elm trees, and from the awesome but beautiful grey stone house. The atmosphere is indigenous. Nowhere else in the world I have as yet encountered can match the excitement and grandeur and couple it with the benevolent warmth of Badminton. It is unique and this is largely attributable to the exceptional man who, every April for the last thirty years, has unselfishly welcomed the world into his back garden. In my own way I like to think that the Duke of Beaufort is akin to a special bottle of port that is never drunk because it is irreplaceable.

Wide Awake's extra-sensory awareness did not miss the magic. He was bristling with well-being but remained relaxed and calm. I often wore draw reins to gallop him, in order to keep him up together. He was inclined to sprawl and I feared that he might strike into himself. He did not need the draw reins at Badminton – he was content to rest quietly on my hands, neck arched, head giving. In the nick of time harmony between us had germinated. We were given five days to savour it.

David had continued to work hard with us both and Wide Awake improved his dressage to lie in third place on the eve of the all-important cross-country day.

Everything looked set. Wakey's legs were in marvellous shape. Nipper's proverbial 'stitch in time' two years ago had done all that he had said it would. Wide Awake now wore a pair of special tendon protectors under his bandages. They did a remarkable job. Light and spongey, they are moulded to the shape of the horse's leg. An impenetrable layer of polyethylene runs between the two layers of softer material for extra protection. Even if the bandage slips or con-certinas, the protectors do not. I have used them on every horse except one, in every three-day event during the past four years and, touching all wood, have not had one bruised tendon.

The steeplechase is my least favourite phase of the three-day event. I ride it worse every year. Wide Awake used to give me some uneasy moments; sometimes loosing-off a stride from the fence and sailing through the air with back hollowed but ears still pricked. Over all ten 'chase fences at Badminton, he did not give me one anxious moment. It was the most lovely steeplechase ride that I have been given by any horse. Such was my confidence that things were going our way, that, most unusually, I remained undaunted when a single magpie flapped across our path on phase C. I blew it a kiss to cancel out the bad luck its presence predicted and told it that Wakey and I would show it how wrong it was.

My mother and Pat Burgess still maintain that Wide Awake's cross-country round was the most inspired that they have seen of any of my rides at Badminton. Provided directions were tactful he allowed me to tell him what to do. He reverted to the ugly hollow jump only once off a turn. No doubt I forgot my legs and used too strong a hand. The erratic jumping, the thoughtless approaches, the casual answers to my questions were no longer in evidence. In their place was a poem, an ecstatic, beautifully scanned and rhythmic poem.

The evening after the cross-country, Annie, wife of the well-known vet Peter Scott-Dunn, gave the leader half an hour of Faradic treatment to loosen up his back muscles. After the cross-country in Ledyard she had discovered that they were stiff and Wide Awake had responded well to her treatment. His back had always been questionable, probably since his car accident. Several people had tried to manipulate it but our own vet, David Watson, seemed to have had the most success with it.

On my way to the final phase of the speed and endurance test, the dance, at midnight that evening, Radio One played Abba's 'San Fernando'. Almost every day that I had driven to Badminton from where we stayed at Wickwar the week's Number One was played. 'San Fernando' became Wide Awake's theme-tune. Turning the radio down as I drew up by the stables, I crept in to ensure that all was well. Jo was there on the stroke of midnight to report that he was fine. He had eaten his two small feeds and a small haynet. She led him out of his stable and trotted him a few yards up the road in the beam of my car headlights. He was sound and his action loose and free. Quickly and quietly he was tucked up in his stable again to resume his all-important sleep. Jo went to bed and I drove to Westonbirt School where the dance was being held.

As I drove I chewed over the wonders of that cross-country day. Wide Awake had gained the fastest clear with 18.8 time faults. To my astonishment the third fastest was dear old George who had competed in his first Badminton the year Be Fair had won. There was something about George that I had always loved. It had struck me then in 1973, that apart from Be Fair, he was the only other horse that I had seen who conformed to my picture of the ideal three-day event horse. At Badminton in 1973 he had gone extremely well, incurring only a technical refusal. The year before he had been the only horse without either time or jumping penalties in the Junior Three-Day Event Championships. Since that Badminton, however, his career had been chequered with falls, and this year he was ridden by a French-Canadian boy instead of his owner's son, Matthew Straker. There was a mysterious rumour about George being rented out for the Montreal Olympics. He had turned in the worst dressage score of 90.83 penalties and his rider, Monsieur Desourdy, had had a 'roll-off' when George pecked badly over the third fence in the cross-country. Despite this and a technical refusal they had earned only 23.2 time penalties. The show-jumping was to add thirty more to their score and leave George in thirtieth place in 1976.

Nick Straker, Matt's older brother, and I were discussing George at the dance. Nick said that George would look after anybody. He had learned to do so whilst hunting in Yorkshire. Then he turned to me and asked, 'Talking of hunting, have you ever had a horse die under you? I had one break its neck under me out hunting two years ago. It was probably the most beastly experience that I have ever had.'

Bending to clasp the leg of the wooden table, I said that I had not suffered similarly. The only death that had faced me was when Risky, my Shetland pony, ate a piece of plastic sack which blocked his intestines. Eventually he had died in Reading Hospital on Palm Sunday, April 11th, 1965.

I did not stay long at the party, but long enough to be asked on three or four separate occasions: 'Which one will you take to Montreal now? Be Fair or Wide Awake? My goodness, you are lucky to have such a choice.'

The thought had momentarily crossed my mind earlier in the evening. It had been easily dismissed. Horses, being horses, have a knack of sorting out such things on their own. It would be made very clear which of those two wonderful horses I would be lucky enough to take to the Olympic Games. 'Who knows?' I thought. 'They might *both* be struck by a falling tree and be out of play by July.'

Nature has a remarkable way of anaesthetising pain. Maybe for this reason I remember very little about that final day's show-jumping. The sun was shining. An impassioned Vicki asked if I thought she looked smart enough, dressed as she was in a trouser suit, should she have to go in to the arena as winning owner and collect the Whitbread Trophy from the Queen.

Wide Awake could not be persuaded to hit a fence in practice. The higher Pat raised the jumps, the deeper Wide Awake dropped his head and neck and the higher he 'basculed' over the top. Wide Awake entered the packed arena with a fence in hand over Hugh Thomas and Playamar. He remained an inspired horse and jumped the most stylish, power-controlled round of his life. He won. And he died. The magpie had been right. Wide Awake had received his award from the Queen, completed his first victory lap and waited to gallop his second. Suddenly he reared up, staggered and fell over backwards. Within forty-five horrifying seconds he was in Heaven. Wide Awake's last tragic surprise was sprung on Palm Sunday, April 11th – eleven years to the day after Risky had died.

No one could discover why he died. Many theorised over some kind of acute heart failure. Just as I will never know how he survived his car accident or why he petrified out hunting, I feel content that the cause of his death shall remain a mystery. It is comforting that not all in life, or in death, can be calculated and explained by human beings.

The sun gave way to blackening skies overhead, and within half an hour of his death they opened with a deluge of rain. Either we curled up in shock and self-pity, or we lived on.

'Let's go and drink champagne. After all he did win and *he* is happy. Let's go and thank him.'

Meanwhile, unasked, fellow competitor Malcolm Wallace, later to become the British team's chef d'équipe, drove the empty 'ice-cream van' home. Sometime later I drove my car home with Mummy. We had not left the village of Badminton before we turned on the car radio and were told by the 6 o'clock news what had taken place at Badminton in the main arena in front of the Queen and thousands of spectators. When we arrived home I found Village Gossip's head looking out of the door that for three years had framed another brown face. In the stable next to him was my four-year-old. For several weeks I had tried in vain to choose a name for him. That evening he was christened – 'Be Brave'.

> Why so kind?
>   Thank you.
> How privileged am I
>   For all that you give me.
> The thrill of achievement
>   Only surpassed by the thrill of communication.
> Just in time
>   Why so kind?
> Just too late
>   Would be most people's Fate.
> Thank you God for such a find.

Seven

Without the kind of mother and father that I had, life that year would have been hard. As it was, it was remarkably easy. It was nothing they said or did, because nothing they said or did changed. Saying and doing are of little help. Just being there is probably the greatest aid. For as long as I could remember my parents had *been* there, ready to help, support, guide and advise. They had never pushed themselves at me. If I did not want advice, they did not offer it, but let me go my own way and learn from my own mistakes.

After Wide Awake's death, they did nothing different. But it was then, in the face of blistering condolences and painful accusations through both the national press and personal correspondence, that I first realised what family strength was. Part of that family strength undoubtedly derived from our mutual love for Be Fair. His presence in the lonely dark hours of the stars was my greatest comfort.

It is but for one reason
That all has been so bearable
That tragedy has not eaten a heart,
It is for Be Fair.
Brilliance does not lend itself
To human definitions.
There are however two examples,
The loss of one still leaves the other
The other has a deep, long-standing love,
It is this that carries me through
This inner knowledge that all is well
With the one loved more than all.

Poor Vicki had no such comfort living on her own in Somerset.

Three months later, Be Fair suffered a rare and crippling injury. He slipped the Achilles tendon off his hock as he finished a superb cross-country round in the Montreal Olympic Games. His competition days were abruptly ended. His life, at least, was spared.

In October, three months after that, Daddy was diagnosed to have terminal cancer. A week later Nanny suffered a sudden and serious heart attack from which she was not expected to recover.

It is almost a law of life that when one door closes, another one opens: a surprise telephone call divided equine and human tragedy. It was about 3 p.m. on Saturday August 14th, three weeks after Montreal. The conversation began in a peculiar way. Ascertaining that he was speaking to me, and without introducing himself, a man's voice asked, 'Do you have a ride at Burghley?'

'No,' I answered. Village Gossip was going to Boekelo at the end of the year instead of Burghley.

'Well, I was wondering if you might like a ride?'

'You bet. Thank you very much for asking me, I'd love a ride. What is the horse?' I was thrilled and felt honoured to be asked only three weeks before Burghley.

'Well, I would rather not tell you the name yet,' he replied.

That appealed to my sense of humour. A complete stranger was ringing me up offering me a ride at Burghley but refusing to tell me which horse it was. Laughingly, I asked, 'Why on earth can't you tell me the name?'

'Well,' replied the voice a little awkwardly, 'because I don't know much about this three-day eventing game; I have more to do with racehorses. The ways are about to part between my present rider and me, I think, and I am testing the ground to see which other riders might be available for Burghley. I just wanted to find out if you were willing to take on the ride, then I can think further, make my decision and let you know either way the day after tomorrow.'

A fleeting doubt sped across my mind. What would happen if I agreed and this man made his decision in my favour, and then I discovered that he was offering me England's most useless or dangerous horse? I ought to find out more if I could.

'Has he been to Badminton or Burghley before, this horse?'

'No, but he has done Tidworth twice, Bramham, Wylye and Punchestown Three-Day Events.'

My mind flashed to Punchestown. Instinctively and without good reason, I was sure that I knew which horse he was talking about. If I was right, this horse, by reputation alone, bordered closely on the useless category.

'Punchestown last year or this?'

'Last year,' replied the voice.

I was even more certain I knew; I had been at Punchestown then.

'How did he go there?' I asked.

'Uh, well, he did not go very well. The rider was sick and they slipped up on a corner of the steeplechase course, and then . . .'

Convinced now that I was right, I did not wait for him to finish but jumped in the deep end and asked: 'Is this horse called Killaire?'

Silence.

'How did you guess?'

'I was at Punchestown last year and remember the trouble.'

I remembered vividly a less than aristocratic bright bay, owned by a mysterious man called Mr Cyzer who did not appear at the competition. Killaire was ridden by a new-comer to the event world, Maribeth Camacho. Only she and her sister, who knew little about horses, were at Punchestown to look after the horse. Maribeth had no help or advice and I remembered discussing the cross-country fences with her beforehand. She had been ill and slipping up on the flat on the steeplechase cannot have helped her state. They fell again on the cross-country course and retired. This, coupled with memories of the scratchy, short-striding manner in which the horse had trotted and can-tered, had left only one impression. Killaire seemed more suited to show-jumping than eventing. But then I remem-bered watching him jump and knew why he had little chance of becoming a show-jumper either.

Charles Cyzer's voice broke into my thoughts.

'Okay, so you are right, but please don't say anything yet. Maribeth and I have had a bit of a disagreement over Killaire and I think that probably the time has come for us to go our separate ways. There are one or two things that have got to be sorted out before the break is made, so please say nothing. But will you take on Killaire if I offer him to you, or should I try someone else?'

I had nothing to lose. Both my top horses were now permanently out of action and Gossip and I did not see eye to eye. My motto had always been 'Ride anything you are offered, however useless, however much of a fool you make of yourself, you will always learn something.'

There was an added and more tricky dimension to this particular situation, however. If you are asked to ride a horse, the civilised course of action is to telephone the ex-jockey and make peace first before agreeing with the owner. In this instance, there was no question of being able to do this. I hardly knew Maribeth but that made it little better. Eventually I replied.

'All right, I'll take him on and have a try. But if he is in no way ready for Burghley, or if we don't get on together, can I reserve the right to send him back to you before?'

'Okay, that's fair. I will telephone you on Monday with my decision. Meanwhile, please say *nothing* to anyone.'

I was bursting to tell someone. Although I was not at all

confident in Killaire's ability, or my own on a strange horse, I was delighted to be presented with a challenge that would give me something other than Montreal to think about. It was the first time that I had been called up at short notice before the big event. This was 'Mark Phillips' style. I felt flattered. I had always longed for this to happen; to see whether or not I could make any sense of the situation. At last the telephone call had come. Secretly I was delighted that it was a rank outsider, most of whose competition results to date had been littered with high dressage scores and many time faults. On such a horse there would be nothing to lose and a bit of fun to be had in the challenge.

In the happiest frame of mind since Montreal, I jumped into my car and drove to Dauntsey to walk the cross-country course for Gossip who was competing there the following day.

My balloon was pricked almost as soon as I started to walk the course. I met Maribeth. An unfortunate coincidence, for we had not seen each other since Punchestown fifteen months before.

Momentarily fazed, I tried to remember that I was supposed to know nothing. I asked her how Killaire was.

'Oh, fine.'

'Is he competing here?' I asked.

'He was, but the owner does not want him to now. He thinks that the ground is too hard.' She paused. 'Quite honestly, I don't know how much longer I will be riding him. Things are not going too smoothly.' Maribeth smiled bravely. She adored Killaire.

'Oh how *awful*.' She could not have known then how sincerely I meant that. It was easy to imagine how I would feel in her place, and in two days' time it looked likely that Killaire would no longer be with her, but with me. 'Hypocrite,' I thought in self-reproach as I wandered on. I hate hiding anything. I would have liked to have told her then and there about the telephone conversation earlier in the afternoon. However, to have said something would have caused more trouble than was already brewing.

Two days later, a bright bay, seemingly about seven months pregnant, backed out of a trailer in Appleshaw's front drive. This was Killaire. An eight-year-old gelding, his sire was the thoroughbred Carnatic; his mother was unknown, but it seemed reasonable to presume that she would have been most useful before tractors were invented. Daddy and I looked at Killaire while Mr Cyzer held him for us.

'How fit is he?' I enquired, somewhat tentatively.

'Oh, he has done quite a bit of work,' he replied.

'Um, he looks as if he will need a bit more if he is going to be fit enough for Burghley – it *is* only three weeks away.' Red warning lights started to flash in my mind. He was soft and fat and looked as if he would need at least six weeks' work before Burghley.

Joanna trotted him once up and down the drive so that we could see if he was sound. He was level, but he moved with short, inelegant steps resembling a tennis player who had borrowed a pair of shoes a size too small for him.

We looked at him again. He possessed a good-looking frame and a big powerful bottom and yet it seemed that he had neither power to jump nor ability to move. Daddy and I were puzzled. Killaire wore a blank expression on his kindly Irish face. There was no spark in his eye; he looked a dull horse.

Before Mr Cyzer departed in his Range Rover and trailer, I mentioned again that if his horse did not go very well for me during the next three weeks, I would send him back. Experiences with Wide Awake and Gossip had left me with little confidence in my ability to acclimatise to a strange horse in a matter of days as opposed to years.

Later that morning I stretched my legs astride this 16.3 table and rode to Toby Balding's field where he has a circular tan training track. On the outside of the track there

63

were a few flights of hurdles. Daddy drove up there to watch us work.

Three weeks until Burghley. I reckoned that Killaire's programme of fitness should have reached a minimum of three six-minute slow canters at this stage, broken by two three-minute intervals of walking.

Killaire was puffing and heaving so much after the first two six-minute canters that he had to be given an extra minute's break and only four minutes for the third canter. When the work had finished, he walked around until he had recovered his breath. Daddy and I wanted to see how he jumped. We thought he could trot over a hurdle to start with. But he could not.

With all due respect, what Killaire did could not be called jumping. He dived at the hurdle as soon as he saw it, legs pounding against the rock-hard ground. Taking two strides to every other horse's one, he skimmed across the top with no inches to spare, landed on the other side and stopped dead. Daddy and I looked at each other. We burst out laughing.

After a few more vain attempts to trot into the hurdle, I pulled him up.

'I don't think he *can* jump big enough to get round Burghley,' I told my father. 'It seems he can only just make two feet eleven.' He gave no feeling of scope whatsoever as, head down, he dived across the fence from its base, propelled off his forehand. After a few consecutive fences I could imagine that he would be doing a headstand up against the face of the jump before he had even taken off.

We wandered home. He was a boring ride, not in any hurry to do anything unless he saw a fence, when he would rush towards it in a mixture of keenness and panic. Three days later we went to a show at the Windsor Park Equestrian Club. This is a marvellous organisation which holds about six shows a year in Windsor Park on Smith's Lawn. There are numerous jumping and dressage classes held to cater for allcomers. Killaire could hardly canter a circle in a proper three-time beat. He was on his forehand and leaned heavily on the bit. If I tried to sit him up off my hand, he became worried and bounced along in four-time. Jumping could not be executed out of a trot, only out of a canter; no matter how many trotting poles were put in front of a fence, he would launch onto his forehand, head well down and scuttle down the poles in some kind of canter.

Our first jumping round in a Foxhunter competition at Windsor Park did nothing to raise my opinion of him. He shuffled hurriedly along, leaning downhill around all the corners. The more I attempted to bounce him and sit him on his hocks before a fence, the faster he bustled into it. He slithered over each one as if he did not want to make an extra inch in height lest that extra inch would hurt him more on landing. He ignored any tactful requests for collection. On the odd occasion when I asked him a little more strongly, he would stop dead in front of the fence. Very soon he delivered one clear message: 'Leave me alone and I will get over – somehow. Mess me about and I will refuse.'

'Somehow' was the operative word. He did not hit his fences like Wide Awake used to. He was careful where he put his legs, but equally unlike Wide Awake he gave no feeling of power and scope. But then how could he without having learned to use his hocks? What spring he had, emanated from his nose and his front feet. His large, potentially powerful bottom was never given a chance to show its worth.

The day after Windsor he was pushed around the tan canter track for three seven-minute canters with two three-minute intervals at walk between them. He worked so badly, with un-eager short pottery strides, that combining this with the jumping experience at Windsor, I did not imagine he could possibly manage Burghley.

He hated the hard ground which his front legs mirrored as they puffed and swelled with the jarring. A horse so much on the forehand as Killaire, during a summer as rainless as that of 1976, was likely to find every stride a sore one. I saw no point in continuing. It seemed unkind to expect this fat waddling hunter to do Burghley. I rang Mr Cyzer and explained my worries and how, apart from being unfit, he hated the hard ground and I suspected he would soon go lame. The tables had turned since Wide Awake's days. Instead of having to persuade the owner to allow me to keep him, I was trying to persuade the owner to take him away. I was very disappointed however at losing the chance of a ride at Burghley and eventually agreed therefore to give him one more chance in three days' time to show some kind of progress during his next fitness work-out.

The whole of a very hot day had been spent trying to show-jump Gossip at the Gillingham and Shaftesbury Show. It did not go well and driving the horsebox home, I felt very depressed. I could not learn how to ride Gossip, and Killaire was not fit to be ridden. I did not think I could be bothered to give Killaire his planned work-out that evening after Gossip and I returned. What was the point? He was too pottery and unfit for Burghley. I thought I would telephone Mr Cyzer that night and arrange to send Killaire home once and for all.

Unenthusiastically, at 7.30 pm on that same warm summer's evening, Killaire began a work-out on Toby's tan. Eventually my conscience had won and I gave Killaire his promised last chance to prove whether or not he was making progress. Surprisingly, he felt lighter on his feet and cantered three eight-minute canters, tiring much less. Mr Cyzer did not receive a call that night and two weeks later, Killaire, looking more slender but no more the picture of an event horse, arrived at Burghley.

Persuading him to trot up in hand for the vets' inspection was the first difficulty. He dragged along behind, ears back, barely raising a jog. It is still very hard to make him trot out in hand. He is terrified of the stick and if one is produced to hurry him up, he bounces sideways away from it rather than forwards.

Like Badminton, Burghley House is surrounded by a magnificent park which possesses its own brand of atmosphere and excitement. The austerity of the Elizabethan architecture and the grandeur of Capability Brown's landscape gardening give rise to a different feeling, but Burghley remains as well organised and as friendly as its spring brother.

Trotting through the park on Killaire, I met Mark Phillips on the hot favourite Persian Holiday. 'What *have* you got there?' He pointed at my hunter.

'Isn't he a joke?' I laughed, trotting beside him. Persian Holiday has a long flowing movement and Killaire seemed to take two and a half strides to every one of 'Percy's'.

'You needn't worry about any competition from this department; he is the slowest horse I've ever sat on,' I said with genuine conviction.

Someone whose opinion is well respected told me later in the day, somewhat crushingly, that if I wanted to stay at the top I had better not waste my time riding this sort of horse. The Irish side of my nature took over, 'Why not?' I thought. 'It is all for fun anyhow.'

It was a wonderful feeling of relief to be riding in a big three-day event on a horse that no one expected to finish anywhere. There were jokes all round about my old hunter. Several other fellow competitors said that they would have to be paid to ride him. 'Isn't he always falling?' It is interesting how one outing, such as Punchestown, can give a horse a bad name. To be fair to Killaire and Maribeth, apart from that incident they had not fallen in two and a half years of eventing. They had merely gone slowly in most of their competitions.

Maribeth came to Burghley to watch Killaire. She held my admiration from that day on, for she turned a potentially awkward situation into a pleasant one. She did not come to visit Killaire in his stable, though, and this I could well understand. In those first three weeks of our association, I had become very attached to him already. He was one of those rare golden people who never looked cross and never said a cross word. He was a seemingly sparkless horse, but there was something very endearing about him, not least his extraordinary method of jumping.

David Hunt had been helping Maribeth with her dressage. Killaire had spent a month with him on his own, the previous year. I can barely imagine what he must have felt like when Maribeth first had him, because apparently he had improved tremendously in the past year since going to David. When he arrived at Appleshaw, he could halt beautifully, always four square, and he could walk, over-bent. He could not trot a horse's gait, only that of a pony, and his canter was a four-beat nose-dive. Dressage riding is my weakest link and probably I did not help the situation either.

David was at Burghley and helped us before our test. Killaire refused to lengthen across the diagonal in the practice arena. Eventually David took the corner boards away and made me trot Killaire across the diagonal and continue out of the arena across the field, kicking every stride until Killaire realised that I was not going to stop asking him to lengthen every time we reached the corner boards. Eventually he made an effort to lengthen his stride, when asked, inside the perimeter of the practice arena.

He was no fool and once in the main arena he knew full well that I would not kick him out over the boards and into the grandstand. He did not bother to show any lengthening. Instead he reverted to running round like a rabbit with his head tucked in. However, he picked up some reasonable marks on his halts and his canters, which had begun to show an improvement by attaining a three-beat pace only on the previous day. Luckily for us it was no vintage year. Dressage performances were poor and an extremely pleasing mark left Killaire in fifteenth place.

That evening Nipper Constance had agreed to come and check Killaire's front legs. I wanted to be certain that his pottery strides were not a warning sign that he was about to break down. Nipper assured me that there was no tendon strain and that his legs were showing only signs of jarring in keeping with many other horses' legs during that equatorial summer of 1976.

The golf course is the usual venue for the steeplechase at Burghley. The afternoon before, it was decided that the burnt grass and the baked clay ground rendered the golf course too hard to use. Three fences were moved to a rotavated field nearby. Inevitably, the heavens opened within an hour of the move. All that night it rained – which was the best possible news for Killaire but the worst for the steeplechase.

Fate had taken a turn in my direction. The rotavated steeplechase course became so deep that it slowed everyone down to Killaire's hen-pace. We picked up twenty-six time faults, the average being about eighteen. It was owing to his tiny scuttle that he was not more heavily penalised on time. His strides were short enough to enable him to hold tightly to the ropes, using the foot-wide strip of unpoached ground between them and the other horses' six-inch-deep tracks. It was difficult to keep up Killaire's enthusiasm. The field was so small that we had to pound around it three times in order to cover the statutory two miles of phase B. Mr Cyzer knew that I would not ask too much of his horse around the steeplechase. He also knew that if Killaire did not recover well on phase C, he would be pulled out before the cross-country.

By the end of phase C he had recovered sufficiently quickly to warrant at least starting the cross-country. The course that year was comparatively short – under four miles. Knowing that he could not be very fit I had no thoughts of making a good time.

Frank Weldon has always said, 'A fast cross-country round is not gained by the speed you go between the fences but by the time you do not waste jumping them.'

Killaire's strides covered so little ground that his speed between the fences was negligible, but he never altered it. He would not decelerate in front of any fence. If anything, he increased his scamper. We had one cross-country practice with Lady Hugh Russell at Wylye, where he indicated once more that if I tried to steady him into a fence, he would stop dead. He confirmed this again shortly before we left Appleshaw for Burghley, when he took an intense dislike to a watertrough in a field. It was barely three foot high, so small that I had steadied him for fear that he might not have noticed it was there.

I did my best to warn him of the unsighted ditch at the bottom of fence number seven, the Coffin, but he paid little attention. His front legs were already over the first set of rails when he saw the ditch and in his surprise he dropped his belly onto the rails, but somehow he kept going. Every fence he jumped was one more than I expected and earned him an appreciative, if surprised, pat.

Capability Brown cut one of the entrance drives to Burghley House ten feet down between two banks. A 2 foot 6 inch palisade sat poised on the summit of one bank. The fence is named Capability's Cutting and owing to the nature of its sharp drop, it must be approached slowly. Killaire pounded in, completely ignoring tentative requests to slow down. He scrabbled over the fence and disappeared into the depths of the drive beneath. Amazingly we emerged intact, but I wondered how many more similar encounters we could survive. It was this novel style which brought Killaire through the finish, recording the third fastest time of the day and moving him up from fifteenth to fifth place.

Azoturia had been an enemy of Killaire's for some time. The first experience we had of him beginning to seize up over his loin muscles was after this cross-country. We kept him walking for three-quarters of an hour, undoing his protective boots and bandages as he moved. The condition thereby subsided before it took a serious hold. It is something that has recurred in a mild form several times since.

The following day he seemed freer in his action as opposed to more jarred. He stood in fourth position by the time the jumping began as poor Welton Samaritan ridden by John Kersley had to withdraw because of leg trouble. Out of the thirty-six horses before him, only a third had gone clear; Killaire had little hope of joining them following our disappointing rehearsal at Windsor. Frank Weldon probably summed it up best when writing in his Burghley report, 'How Killaire ever got round the third day jumping unscathed, I shall never know, because whatever he did, it certainly was not show-jumping.'

To be in the leading position at the end of the cross-country and then make a mistake in the show-jumping, must be the worst way to lose a three-day event. Equally, most will agree, it is the worst way to win one. However, it does happen and it happened at Burghley. Poor Toby Sturgis had two fences on the floor and Sandy Brookes knocked one down. Before we realised it, Jane Holderness-Roddam had won with Warrior and Killaire was runner-up. As he and Warrior stood alone out in front of the double row of competitors for the prize-giving, Mr Cyzer reappeared from behind the temporary grandstands where he had buried his face in the canvas in preference to watching his horse trying to show-jump. He watched the prize-giving and when he heard the commentator announcing his rider's credentials he turned to his wife Annie and exclaimed, 'Good God, I didn't know she had won Badminton twice! I would never have dared to ring her up and ask her to ride Killaire if I'd known that.'

That weekend was responsible for another remarkable character change in a horse. Killaire came home to Appleshaw for a few days before returning to his Sussex home. He was in robust health, proud and definitely pleased with himself. This could have been attributable to the adrenalin, released by the big occasion, but Killaire has never looked back since. He has never again been a dull dormouse, slopping along the roads. In a short time Killaire became the horse I loved most after Be Fair. Not because I expected him to bring great triumph, he would not; but because he did not have a nasty thought in his head.

My affections had not been able to find a wide enough chink in Gossip's armour. He was an individual who lived alone on 'Treasure Island'. He was as reserved in accepting affection as he was in giving it. He seemed almost masochistic. If he kicked someone who then kicked him back, he would put his ears forward and look contented. Gossip possesses probably as much talent and treasure on his island as any other horse I shall be lucky enough to sit on. Sadly I have still not discovered a permanent mooring for my boat. Frequently he welcomes me on short visits to whet my appetite and then cuts me loose into the ocean of despair once again. It is my failure. There is a way to every horse.

A month after Burghley, Jo and I made our way to Holland again. This time with Village Gossip. He completed a fast cross-country but crumpled inexplicably as he landed over the Normandy Bank. Boekelo had shown that he was not ready for Badminton next year. We were not sufficiently in unison. He was fighting everything I did. In some respects, I thought maybe it was Wide Awake all over again – a highly strung, hot-blooded edition. Like Wakey, he detested pressure on his mouth. Whereas Wakey would hit the fence, if he felt too much pressure, Gossip would refuse it. I dared not release too much of the pressure on Gossip's mouth, however. He galloped at such a fantastic speed into a fence if I did let go, that I feared he would cartwheel over it. Many bits stronger than a snaffle were tried, but once again mechanics were not going to provide the answer. The problem lay in his tightly winched mind, as did the secret to

9a. An inspiration. Badminton. (*Peter Harding*)

9b. George behaves like a gentleman
in his dressage. Badminton, 1977. (*Thomas Noel*)

10. Killaire's steeplechase was hard work.
Badminton, 1977.

11a. Approaching the bounce fence into the lake, completely unconvinced of its feasibility . . .

11b. . . . Killaire squeezed in a tiny stride and popped neatly over the second rail. Badminton, 1977. (*Thomas Noel*)

12a. George takes me safely through the bounce into the lake . . . (*John Elliot*)
12b. . . . and makes an ingenious recovery after the bank gave way on take-off at the Trakehner. Badminton, 1977. (*Peter Harding*)

13a. Riding George and leading Killaire in the parade –
a superb thrill. Badminton, 1977. (*Leslie Lane*)

13b. Somehow Killaire managed to clear the remaining eight
fences. Badminton, 1977. (*Thomas Noel*)

14.
In admiration.
George, Badminton, 1977.
(*Peter Harding*)

15. Elaine Straker leads home George, her newly acclaimed Badminton champion. (*John R. Corsan*)

16a.
I heard what Richard said as he briefed me for the cross-country, but I could barely take it in.
Burghley, 1977.

16b. Not the usual fun this time. George tackles the cross-country. Burghley, 1977. (*John Elliot*)

controlling him.

Having decided not to let Gossip run at Badminton, 1977, I was delighted when Charles Cyzer asked me to ride Killaire. Unabashed by Burghley there was no reason why Killaire should not progress to Badminton. I was sceptical about his peculiar jumping habits, however, and wondered if Badminton would not find him out.

Since Burghley, I had been told several tales regarding Killaire's lack of esteem when he was eventing and show-jumping as a four- and five-year-old in Northern Ireland. Horsy stories should not always be believed, but Killaire's tale was repetitive in its detail. It seemed he had not had enough scope to show-jump properly and may have been over-faced, when he was tried, which possibly accounted for the way he held the whip in such terror. He was then redirected to eventing where, it seemed, he spent a certain amount of his time on the floor, until one day he managed to qualify for the Scarva Open Championships. He won these and was sold to England on the strength of it. Such rumours of falling were not to be taken too seriously I felt, especially as they referred to four years past. In the back of my mind, however, they could not fail to leave an imprint. It worried me that Badminton might test his limit and his scope too far, he might become frightened and revert to finding solace on the floor.

Eight

Shortly before Christmas, Matthew Straker rang up. 'I'll come straight to the point,' he said. 'Would you like to ride George at Badminton?'

My instinctive reaction was 'No'. Five 60 penalties that he had been accorded in the past four years shot through my mind. I had witnessed two of the falls, both of them at last fences. Reports of a dreadful fall that he had sustained at Burghley had even filtered out to Russia, during the European Championships at Kiev in 1973. From then on his fortunes at the 'Big Bs' were shaky and his reputation shook likewise.

And yet there had always been something about George that I had liked and admired.

Mark Phillips had been George's reserve jockey on several occasions when both Matt and Nick were abroad with the Army. I wondered why he had not been asked to ride George at Badminton.

It soon became apparent that he had been asked first, but was overloaded with three rides for Badminton '77 already.

My sense of challenge was welling up fast. How thrilling to be asked to ride another strange horse so soon after the excitement of Killaire.

Feeling that the matter ought to be discussed with my parents, I thanked Matt very much and said I would ring back the next day.

'You are *not* riding George at Badminton!' was my poor mother's first remark as I put the telephone down.

'No, don't worry. I'm not – yet.'

I telephoned Mark to discuss George. He was encouraging, and although he said that he had not ridden him for a couple of years he felt that George was a very good horse.

Daddy was already seriously ill by that December. His jerseys and trousers hung off him. None of us admitted it, but we all knew that he was dying. With courage, typical of a man of his stature, he lived for the future. We all did. This, I am sure, had a certain amount to do with the alacrity with which both he and Mummy decided to stand behind me in my desire to try and ride George at Badminton. Provided he was permitted to leave Yorkshire and spend the spring with us at Appleshaw, we agreed it was worth a go – for fun.

This I knew would be the stumbling block. Like Mr Cyzer, Mrs Straker likes to look after her own horses and not send them away. As an owner myself I fully understand this, but as a jockey it is my neck that is at risk in a big three-day event on a horse which is a complete stranger. It is not because I think that the horse will necessarily be looked after any better at Appleshaw, but because I must familiarise myself with him – learn what mood he is in, what attitude to life he has; learn how to adjust his programme in the last vital few weeks according to whether he is working with gaiety or with boredom. Just as I believe that the largest part of successful riding lies in the mind, equally I believe that a horse will give his best only if his mind and body are content, and in harmony with his rider.

Later in December, a four-hour train journey north eventually took me to Little Hutton near Darlington, where I was to ride George and see if we liked each other.

He was as perfect a three-day eventer to look at as I had remembered him to be. A 16.2 h.h., strong, beautifully proportioned, big-limbed brown horse. He was home bred out of the Strakers' mare Winnifrith (by the winner of the 1948 Grand National, Sheila's Cottage). His sire was the thoroughbred St Georg, later shipped to Germany. His wise, generous eyes portrayed his character. The ground was frozen hard in the afternoon when Nick on his young horse Barclay took George and me out for our initial acquaintance. George must have slipped on take-off at the first small fence we jumped. He made a blunder, hitting it with one front leg as he screwed over. 'Great beginning,' I thought, quietly smiling to myself.

By the end of our jumping ride, I was definitely aware of George's exceptional abilities. Despite a surprise refusal at a hedge, I reckoned he must be more than capable of taking me round Badminton. The challenge would lie in whether or not he would keep upright.

After lengthy discussion and a good deal of give and take on both sides, Mrs Straker agreed to send George down to Appleshaw in the spring, five weeks before Badminton.

Returning from three weeks' dressage with top German professional rider Herbert Rehbein in Hamburg, I was summoned to Yorkshire to ride George. The Strakers had organised an evening of equine entertainment in their indoor school and we were supposed to perform a solo dressage display as one of the acts. In a double bridle and wearing tail coat and top hat, George and I ambled through the FEI test during a sub-zero February night. Neither of us added much enlivenment to the evening.

Meanwhile Killaire had begun to change shape and manner of carrying himself after spending a month with David. Remarkably he had learnt the foundations of extended trot. It took another eighteen months before he had the strength and correctly placed balance to produce a reasonable extension.

Killaire came home two months before Badminton. He had maintained his Burghley personality. Despite this he remained the safest horse to ride out at Appleshaw.

George came to us in mid-March. In his suitcase he brought only his pyjamas, two pairs of brushing boots and a spare set of shoes. Lisa, who had come four months earlier to replace Joanna, searched with me for some pills or powders which we thought George might be taking. We found nothing.

To this day I remain aghast at the destructive power of rumour. For some time hearsay alone had implied that George was not a sound horse and that he was probably living on painkillers.

The Strakers had assured me that he was neither lame nor sustained by powders. It is a salutary lesson not to listen to ill-disposed gossip that George proved to be fundamentally sound all spring while living off nothing more than oats, nuts and hay.

During the first week of our association we went several times to Pat Burgess for help with our jumping. Neither of us was particularly encouraged by George. He jumped without enthusiasm and tended to veer left down the small athletic grids.

His physique worried me. He seemed to be losing rather than gaining bloom and lustre. Maybe he was homesick. He had always looked extremely well whenever I had seen him in the past. He was zestless and the vet gave him a tonic. During the second week I decided to give him a few days off to see if he would pick up some spirits and condition. He was shod at the beginning of the third week by Mr Linssner, our faithful and hardworking blacksmith. That day Mr Linssner made one of his very few errors and pricked George, so rest was forcibly continued for another ten days. During this period George went three times to swim in the Lambourn pool to try and keep him fit, and eventually I put him 'on the box' to see if faithhealing helped his general condition. It was worrying that he was not having enough work and might never be fit enough for Badminton. However some consolation was found in the thought that maybe my Saviour was looking after me again and preventing George from going to Badminton at all. He was sound two days before Brigstock. Without either show-jumping or cross-country practice he took me into the advanced class there. On the strength of a long cold winter of hard work that his owner and breeder, Elaine Straker, had put into him herself, he won it. No one was more staggered than me, for by then I had more or less given up the idea of Badminton and taken him to Brigstock mainly because there was no good reason for him to stay at home.

We are forever in Mr Linssner's debt. The extra ten-day break that George enjoyed rekindled his spark and prevented him from being over-done by practising things which he already knew how to do, and which consequently bored him.

George was twelve years old in 1977 and he had been three-day eventing for five years. Fortunately he needed little work to attain peak fitness, and two work-outs between Brigstock and Badminton rendered him fresh and ready for the attack. My confidence in him had been enormously swelled by Brigstock.

Killaire had enjoyed an uninterrupted programme and had raced round Rushall with his mouse-like strides to record third in the advanced class. He was a completely different horse from George. One was the bold-striding, quick-thinking, class event horse on whom it was possible to give normal directions; the other was a tiny striding, quick-thinking class hunter on whom it was best to give no direction at all.

Two horses at Badminton need at least one experienced person looking after them, and Joanna came back to show Lisa, her replacement, the ropes.

I wondered if the inspiration that Badminton infused would still be in evidence when I rode into the Park on the first day. It was possible that it may have died with Wide Awake the preceding year.

The inspiration lived on. Badminton still made me feel happier than almost anywhere else. Nature had most effectively pulled down the blinds on last year. At the beginning of the week the press did their best to roll them back up again. By mid-week they deemed it imprudent.

If lucky enough to have two horses in a three-day event, deciding which to ride first can be difficult. To ride the best horse last will, in most competitions, give him a greater chance, as the rider can draw from the experience gained on the first. However, if the less good one is ridden first there is a chance of injury and missing altogether the ride on the better horse. There was not a great deal to choose between my two for Badminton 1977. Both were uncertain. It seemed fairest to Charles to make Killaire number one as I had ridden him for longer than George.

The first day's dressage left Killaire lying in third place. He had tried hard. It was a welcome change from Be Fair, Wide Awake or Gossip, to ride into the Badminton dressage arena on a predictable and even-natured horse.

George was number 69 and went near the end of the second day. The atmosphere was tense but George continued to behave like a gentleman. He too was an obedient, placid horse, and after my helpful visit to Germany I found he was not difficult to ride. He overhauled his stablemate, and cut his own previous year's mark by nearly two-thirds. With a score of 37.4 he stood fourth overall, while Killaire held tenth place with 47.4.

Cross-country day dawned bright. Small, fluffy white clouds broke up the clear blue sky. The car parks filled throughout the morning with hundreds of vehicles that had snaked their way down the congested Gloucestershire lanes. Over a hundred thousand people spread themselves across the Great Park. Amongst them was the Appleshaw Supporters' Club. Mr Cook is as much a part of Appleshaw as the front door. He does everything, building stables and cross-country fences as thoroughly as he used to milk the cows and tend the calves. At first he came to Badminton in a car, but now with the growing enthusiasm of his large family of children and grandchildren, his flock come to Badminton (and every other accessible event) in a car and a mini-bus. Mr Linssner did not join the Cooks' party this year – owing to his family's increasing interest he had to take his own car.

At mid-day Killaire was opening the batting. Never before had I gone first in a major competition. A great deal of my previous fortune had come through being drawn late and benefiting from other people's experiences. Without great confidence in either of my horses I was more nervous than ever on cross-country morning. Maybe this accounted for stepping out of the horsebox in my boots but having forgotten to put on my breeches.

Killaire's steeplechase was hard work – it always will be, because he is not a fast horse. Most horses find that their normal galloping stride is fast enough to be inside the time on the steeplechase without trying too hard. Poor Killaire, as usual, had to go flat out for the whole two miles. It is no fun asking a horse to give his all, especially when there are still six miles of roads and tracks and four and a half miles of cross-country in front of him.

It was nerve-racking setting out on the cross-country. First to go and on a horse who had yet to prove that he had sufficient scope and ability. As usual I sat on the loo during the ten-minute break in the Box before the start of the cross-country, wondering why I had *ever* started eventing in the first place. Be Fair received the blame, once again. For the amount of times he receives the blame, however, the gratitude accorded him is four-fold.

Most competitors who have not begun phase A, crowd into the small tent in the Box to watch the closed-circuit television of the cross-country. It is always interesting to watch the fate of the first few horses and riders and see if any lessons can be learned.

It was the first time that a bounce fence had been built on the edge of the lake. No one knew whether it was possible to expect a horse to jump one stout post and rails, land, and take straight off over a second when the landing, six foot lower down, was into water. There was an alternative, but it was slower and equally unappetising. Either the bounce was possible or it was not and the sooner we found out the better.

Killaire lined up for the Lake and for once listened to my request to slow down. A few strides out I saw a vivid image in my mind of fellow competitors crowded round the television eagerly waiting to see if bouncing into the lake was practicable or not. The water sparkled in the sun; maybe it would not be too cold. The hushed crowds behind the crush barriers were some twenty deep. There was only the sound of Killaire's scampering hoof beats. Holding him between hand and leg and sitting up straight to help keep us both balanced, I had time to wonder what little treat might be in store for all those thousands of eyes that were watching. It is the only fence that I have approached in all my life completely unconvinced of its feasibility.

In the space of fifteen feet between the two rails, Killaire squeezed in one of his tiny strides and popped neatly over the second rail and splashed down into the lake. He bounced out of the water, up the bank at an angle and over the sleeper wall. He cantered away up the hill leaving the crowd to sing his praises. He realised he was going away from home again and slowed a little. I felt he must be tiring and being so grateful for his masterly handling of the Lake fences, did not push him much thereafter.

We endured only one nasty moment on the whole course which was entirely my fault. Approaching the corner of the Vicarage Vee, suddenly he felt as if he had lost impulsion. Instead of kicking harder, I hit him. He hated the stick and I knew it, but it was my reflex action. He veered sharply left-handed away from it as he took off. There was plenty of time to repeat some silent and rude self-recriminations as he aimed head first for the bottom of the angled ditch. There could be no escape. I had stepped into that boggy ditch myself the day before. The mud in its bottom had come over the top of my boots. Incredibly, Killaire managed to jump into and out of the ditch as if it was part of the intended obstacle and with barely a stumble continued, unflustered, on his way. No one will ever know how he did it, as indeed in my mind we had already fallen.

Killaire thus proved himself a Badminton horse. He demonstrated ample scope but rarely gave an inch more than was needed. I was certain he could never win a major three-day event – he just could not go fast enough – but he was honest and genuine and would always try his best. Those assets were to prove to be of inestimable value in the future.

There was an hour between finishing Killaire's round and starting out on George. I lay flat out above the cab of the horsebox and willed myself to sleep. One horse is tiring enough, I had never tried to ride two before. In a semi-conscious state, I heard rain beating down on the roof above my nose. The weather had broken. What a nuisance, slippery going for George was not going to help him keep his feet.

There was a bellow from outside the horsebox. 'Lucinda, for God's sake wake up will you? It is time to get on George.'

Daddy sounded cross. I could not understand why; I had only been asleep a few minutes. Then I remembered how ill he was. He must already be exhausted, but he was not going to give up. He was determined to play his part in the Box with George, just as he had done with Killaire and with Be Fair, Wide Awake, Ellie May, Hysterical and Gossip before him.

Whether I now ride steeplechase worse because of George or whether George went worse because of me, I do not know. However it was a scaring experience and not even Wide Awake in his earliest, most erratic days hit the fences like George did. When he was on the correct stride he jumped well. When he was wrong he appeared to make no effort to shorten or adjust his stride. Instead he used the ground-board like a step-off as he ploughed through the fence, birch flying. He took the guard rail of the Open Ditch with him across the fence and the following competitor had to be held up while the fence was repaired. Somehow we did not fall but he leaned hard left all the way which stole some of my valuable energy in keeping him straight. It also took some guesswork. The rain lashed horizontally into my eyes and at 690 metres a minute the best thing to do is to close them. I think possibly George closed his too.

For forty minutes we trotted and cantered down phase C through a blanket of incessant rain. Sun makes me feel brave, rain has the opposite effect. The confidence in George acquired after Brigstock had evaporated with the experience on the steeplechase. Maybe this was what he did at the big competition. Maybe he just switched off and galloped through the fences . . . By the time George and I arrived back in the Box at the end of phase C, I was genuinely frightened of what lay ahead. Four and a half miles and with about forty-five fixed, solid, questioning obstacles. The rain had soaked through two jerseys and my stretch breeches flapped soggily against my legs. I was cold and shivering. Slipping and sliding around in my saddle at the rising trot I saw little hope of staying in it if George acknowledged the cross-country fences in the manner in which he had treated the steeplechase fences. In the Box I asked Daddy to make sure of two things: firstly that the dry spare saddle was put back on George and not the wet, flabby saddle that had been taken off him before he was washed down. Secondly that an extra thick layer of Vaseline was smeared down the front of all four legs. This perhaps would give him a little more chance of sliding instead of falling over the fences when he hit them. Unsticking my string gloves from my fingers I tottered, freezing cold, to the usual haven of peace. I was too cold to stay still long, so came out and went to have a word with Elaine, George's owner. The Lake fences really worried me. I did not believe George would take enough trouble at the bounce. Certain that he would hit it and fall into the water, it seemed better for him to jump through the alternative route. Elaine feared he would overjump the alternative and be in trouble as he landed in the dragging weight of the water. She assured me that he would do the bounce all right as Killaire had done. I did not believe her, but she knew George infinitely better than me, having bred and trained him. Eventually I decided that whichever way I went he would fall, so it had better be her fault and not mine.

My fingers were wet and numb. They did not seem to have enough control over themselves to struggle into a dry pair of Nanny's specially knitted string gloves. Gradually I was going numb all over, starting with my brain. At that point Daddy, with effort, legged me up and walked George towards the start box, 'Good luck, old girl. Don't forget you *do* do it for fun.'

Obviously he had not missed the turmoil that was going on inside me. Nor had Elaine – she grabbed my knee, 'I promise you, Lucinda, he'll look after you. Don't worry, he has hunted for years and knows it all backwards. Just go out there and enjoy the hunt. He'll look after you. He *is* brilliant.'

She genuinely believed in George's ability. It was the conviction in her voice which exploded me out of that paralysis, and made me believe that George would indeed look after me.

It was an unrepeatable ride. I do not think George made one mistake. Like Killaire, he popped in a tiny neat stride between the bounce fences in front of the lake, leaving in me a feeling of guilt that I had doubted his prowess. He was ingenious in his recovery at the Trakehner which had claimed several victims shortly before him. The bank had started to give way on the take-off and horses were beginning to slip into the ditch and under the rail. It gave way with George too but despite this his extraordinary dexterity, indeed his brilliance, took him over the top of the rail instead of underneath it.

Only George and The Kingmaker, ridden by Diana Thorne (now Henderson), finished with no time penalties. Dividing those two on the scoreboard was Carawich and Aly Pattinson. Killaire lay a close fourth with 13.2 time penalties to add to his dressage score.

Phase E, the dance, had still to be attended, though that night only briefly. Elation and relief are sustaining for a long time but not forever.

The parade of the surviving Badminton competitors takes place in the main arena at 2.30 pm on the afternoon following the cross-country day. The competitors parade at walk around the arena in numerical order, the commentator in the meantime reading out identification, rank and honour of each competitor in turn.

It was a superb thrill to walk into that arena riding Number 69, George, and leading Number 1, Killaire. Neither of these numbers could in any way be related to the lucky number seven. While riding the leader and leading the fourth best, the answer to the superstition suddenly revealed itself: 69 plus 1 equals 70 – what luckier number?

Both Killaire and George behaved immaculately. With their ears pricked, they knew exactly how important they both were. I am afraid neither Be Fair nor Wide Awake could have found similar alert composure. They each maintained this marvellous tranquillity when they worked for twenty minutes before jumping. George was more supple, flexible and harmonious than he had been all spring. Like Wide Awake the year before, he jumped better than ever outside, refusing to touch a pole. Killaire was not as good as George but he was more settled and easier than usual. He had knocked one fence down in every round he had jumped since our fluke clear at Burghley. He still bombed into his fences leaving the springboard, his hocks, far out behind him. I had tried a Kimblewick bit, show-jumping at Rushall, and it had made it easier to balance his headlong approach. I very nearly decided to use it on the cross-country at Badminton but after what happened while wearing it in the show-jumping, it was lucky he remained in his snaffle and cavesson noseband. He jumped the first three fences suffering the indignity of the Kimblewick's control. At the fourth fence he stopped dead. A reflexive whack from my stick propelled him over from where he stood. He cleared that one, but he was so upset by his whack that he smashed through the next. His message reverberated around the arena's packed stands: 'For goodness sake, leave me alone.' I obeyed and he scuttled off, head down, somehow managing to clear the remaining eight fences.

There was little time to worry about how badly I had ridden. Quickly weighing-in after Killaire had finished, I climbed onto George and we went over to the practice fence where Dick Stillwell, trainer and old friend, had promised to meet us and give us last-minute advice and confidence. I never remember exactly what he says or does but he has the indefinable knack of holding the pieces together when the tension is threatening to disintegrate them.

Although George cantered into the arena with three fences in hand, apprehension was rife as he had disposed of three the previous year. However with the deftness of a master he jumped a round worthy of one of the best three-day event horses in the world. It was St George's Day – the patron saint of England was smiling on his namesake's only celebrated offspring.

My admiration of his quality and relentless generosity is infinite. After five years and five different riders he could have been excused if he had felt a little jaded. But he did not. He gave his very best. His very best, I believe, would be unbeatable by anyone in the world.

George and Elaine received their due reward from the Queen, for the twelve years of care and training they had put in together and which had served to give me a third Whitbread Trophy.

Killaire, placed third, galloped the victory lap alongside George. I wonder if he felt a trifle indignant at being led around the main arena. Perhaps he resolved then and there never to let it happen again.

It was wonderful that Daddy could witness this for it was something that none of us would have been naïve enough to dream could happen.

Whitbread's allowed me to take home 'The George' which they had hung outside their inn sign exhibition – if I was able to fetch it down from where it swung.

Six days later I fell off cloud nine, literally. Approaching a sleeper table at Locko Park One-Day Event, too fast and unbalanced, poor Hysterical hit it above both her knees. The point-to-point collar bone caught the punishment due me and I was towed off to the first-aid tent by some bored-looking St John's Ambulance ladies. Bored, I think, because mine was not the first collar bone of the afternoon. This, their third case, nearly became a compound fracture. I was led round the edge of the tent to receive attention. No one was supporting me and still slightly dazed, I tripped over the guy ropes and fell shoulder first straight onto the broken collar bone. I found it quite funny, even then, remembering my scant teaching in home nursing, 'Keep hold of the patient.'

It was not that funny though and I had been sitting down for only a few seconds when, for the first time in my life, a Hollywood-style faint enveloped me.

Neither George nor Killaire was at Appleshaw to share the celebrations after Badminton. Carrots and packets of Polos, sent to them from thoughtful admirers, had to be redirected. It was sad to be without them in the happy aftermath of that great moment, but it was a small price to pay for being lucky enough to ride someone else's precious horses.

It was less than a year since Wide Awake and Be Fair had

had their careers prematurely ended. 'Something good comes out of every evil.' Something good, for me at least, was George and Killaire. I had always longed to be asked to ride someone else's advanced horse to see if it was possible. It is rare for a horse not be firmly anchored to his rider once he has painstakingly climbed the ladder to advanced standard. The British Army was to be thanked for George. It had forbidden Matthew Straker appropriate leave from Cyprus to ride at Badminton that year.

Nine

Both George and Killaire spent ten days with David Hunt in mid-July, whilst Gossip and I, accompanied by an old friend, William Micklem, invaded Germany. On the way to the three-day event at Luhmühlen, we spent a week with Herbert Rehbein. The usual humiliation was suffered. Gossip performed impeccable dressage for Herbert and continued to go like a taut goose for me. Herbert loved him and had Gossip been bigger Herbert said he would have liked him as his own dressage horse – the final accolade to my capabilities as a dressage rider. I still cannot put him securely on the bit when away from home. With typical kindness Herbert lent me his own saddle for Luhmühlen. It was so well moulded to his wonderful seat that I must have looked a great deal more impressive than usual. One of the foreign judges, a German, was dazzled to such a degree that he gave us twenty marks more than either of his fellow judges. At the end of the dressage, Gossip lay fifth with an unmerited low score of penalties. German Olympic bronze medallist, Karl Schultz, told the press that my score was 'completely crazy'. If it was not amended he threatened to take both his horses out of the competition and leave Luhmühlen. No one seemed to mind much if he did. He stayed, and so did Gossip's mark. The unfortunate judge was accused of Anglophilia, and, fearing his compatriot's anger, he dared not appear at the party that night.

Since then Gossip has more than paid for this moment of generosity. By the end of the following year, his reputation preceded him into the arena and he began to earn some fairly vindictive scores.

Gossip's speed across country assured him of second place despite an appallingly spooky show-jumping round. I still had not learned that he liked to do everything on his own, even show-jumping, on an unrestrained rein at great speed.

We arrived back at Appleshaw from Germany by Tuesday lunchtime. That afternoon, I drove to David's to ride Killaire and George before the Three-Day Event Dressage Championships to be held the following day at Wembley.

Killaire delighted me but George did not. He felt inanimate and old. As usual he did everything that was asked of him but he felt stiffer and there was no gaiety left in his stride.

Mummy came down to David's from London to see the three of us. She had not come to Luhmühlen because Daddy was too ill. He was in hospital in London and we went to see him that evening. He told me how thrilled he was that Gossip had gone so well in the three-day event in *Italy*. I knew then that he would not be with us for long.

The following day was the annual non-event for me. Only once in the past seven years have I not been in the bottom handful at the Wembley Three-Day Event Dressage Championships. This year was no exception. To my astonishment, Killaire exploded with joy at being released from David's indoor school. It was lovely to know he was feeling so well after Badminton. George on the other hand dragged himself through the test and was nearly thrown out by the judges for being unsound. He never felt completely right on his off-fore all that autumn. The problem maybe resembled Wide Awake's as he used to pull out stiff and then work sound. Possibly the uncomfortable jump at the Badminton Trakehner in April had wrenched some deep-seated muscle.

Two weeks later they both did the dressage and show-jumping phases of the Dauntsey One-Day Event. Killaire was beginning to enjoy himself thoroughly in the dressage but not because he was doing it well. Like all my horses, except dear, kind, patient George, he had discovered that I was not especially adroit at this discipline. He knew the FEI test by heart and knew exactly when to do the extended canters across the diagonal. He would set off round the corner, building up momentum and tilting onto his forehand to ensure that I had no control as he scampered as fast as he could across the arena. In order that he did not jump the arena boards in the far corner I had to lean back and pull extremely sharply. In retaliation he would buck, change legs and jolt hastily to a halt almost simultaneously. None of these movements were part of the required repertoire.

The following day Killaire started to cough. His stable was not near George's at home but they had just spent a week in adjoining stables at Wylye during team-training for the European Championships to be held at Burghley in September.

Killaire was laid off for six weeks and withdrawn from the Midland Bank Advanced One-Day Event Championships and final team trial at Locko. We all knew the effects of galloping a horse too soon after he had been coughing. Anything can happen, from a slightly strained heart or lungs to a strain severe enough to stop one or the other functioning altogether.

We waited anxiously during the two weeks leading up to Locko fearing that we might hear George start to cough as well. George did not become sick but two days before Locko Daddy died.

Lisa, George and I trudged on up to Locko in Derbyshire and Simon, my brother, followed the next day, in support.

Most of my friends were wonderful, but the faces of a few were unforgettable as they stared at me in horror. It had not struck me before that some people genuinely believe in mourning. Our family has always tried never to look back, only forwards. Certainly I find it the best way to cope with grief.

Since March I had stopped eating. Living off apples and cheese I was stricken with the desire to suffer in order to become thin and elegant. As the year wore on I became progressively thinner and weaker but certainly no more elegant. Despite the daily fitness routine of 300 skips becoming noticeably more tiring I remained convinced that I was fitter and stronger than I had ever been.

George actually ran away with me at Locko. He came crashing out of the wood through the Bullfinch and into the bright sunlight and full view of the spectators, including his horrified owner and my brother Simon. The yellow silk flew off my crash hat as he tore down the hill relentlessly leaning against the unnoticed haul on the reins. A merciful uphill stretch followed but then a sharp descent to a fence at the river's edge which had to be jumped slowly out of trot. The television picked up a weakened, appealing cry. 'Stop, George, please stop. *George, will you please stop!*' as a brown horse and a pale yellow rider, weaving from left to right, galloped down towards the river and the camera. The rider was making little impression in her attempts to slow the horse. When George leaned he leaned very heavily and much strength was needed to rebalance him in front of a fence. Although this had been necessary before only two fences at Badminton, at Locko it seemed to be needed at nearly all of them. Somehow we completed the cross-country unpenalised.

Feeling anaesthetised I fell asleep in the horsebox before the show-jumping and felt so ill on waking that I could barely crawl onto George. Maybe this was a good preparation for what he was going to have to cope with at the European Championships at Burghley in a fortnight's time. He looked after me and maintained his second place in the Midland Bank Championships behind Mark Phillips and Persian Holiday.

Selfishly I was thankful that Killaire's cough had prevented him competing at Locko as well. By the law of averages two rounds ridden like that one could never have escaped accident.

Ten

George arrived at Burghley four days before the European Championships were due to begin. He seemed bored and disinterested. He could derive no spark from me as I felt ill and slept each and all afternoon. I walked the cross-country very early in the morning before the crowds arrived, and before I might start to feel peculiar again. The course did not inspire me, but then that was probably my fault not the course builder's. None of it really frightened me enough to ensure that I rode my best. On the other hand, the very fact that I was *not* worried rendered me sufficiently respectful of it.

Friday was dressage day. At 7.15 a.m. Colonel Bill Lithgow, for a decade the highly successful British chef d'équipe, picked me up and drove me from the George Hotel to the cross-country course.

For the third and final time I walked every blade of grass that hopefully George would tread. I recorded a few interviews with English and European journalists, which during the last few days had served to remind me that I was in fact defending my European Championship title, which Be Fair had won in Luhmühlen in 1975. Normally it is a fight to push away such pressurising thoughts. This time it was no problem. They slipped back into the dimness of my unimpassioned mind as easily as they had escaped.

Over half of the course had been walked as I wandered down the slope from the Hayrack. On the right stretched the great lake, at one end of which stood the turreted castle, Burghley House. For a moment the burden lifted. I felt happy. In the water of the lake the early morning sun reflected the bluest of skies. No one else was about. There was no sound. Surrounded by the peaceful mystery of the park's ancient trees I felt a sense of genuine pride. Here, in England, a country for which people often made apologies to their visitors, was an immovable relic of the glorious, invincible heritage which we British enjoy. For several minutes I stood still, absorbing the peace and the magnificence. The complications of walking the cross-country course for the European Championships diminished proportionately when compared to the skills of the men who had fashioned such beauty.

I squelched on. My gym shoes had been soaked through since fence three, the Leaf Pit. The dew within them had warmed to blood temperature around my feet. They felt like a pair of thermally insulated shock absorbers. Walking in rubber boots on the first day had produced instant blisters.

George felt lifeless that morning. Elaine advised me not to school him but to take him instead for a gay 'hunting' ride. We galloped across stubble fields, leaped hedges, popped over rails. George jumped cleanly and cheerfully. An hour later a happy horse waltzed back to his stable. He ate his lunch and Lisa began his hairdressing session. Meanwhile I changed into top hat, tail coat, breeches and boots, pondering all the time what to do with George before his test. It seemed that, in contrast to any other horse I had ridden, he was going to require livening up for his dressage. I was not quite sure, however, what sort of electrifying effect the arena might have on him, although I had a suspicion that, such was his mood at the moment, he would not notice whether he was surrounded by a packed grandstand or a thicket of trees. Taking a chance, he was left in his stable until twenty minutes before his test.

With girths tightened but stirrups at long dressage length I set sail from the stable area at a strong canter and on the way pointed George at a couple of practice cross-country fences and a show-jump. As we flashed through the park perimeter gate and cantered up towards the main arena, I caught sight of my mother laughing out loud to herself. It probably *was* an amusing sight: tail coat flying, hand anchoring top hat, as George leaped big solid timber fences.

After ten minutes of small circles and transitions under the eye of our team trainer, the Spanish Riding School artist Ernst Bachinger, George cantered quietly into the ring. He did notice that the grandstands housed people and not trees. He became a little more lively: enough for me to ride him with impulsion but not enough to prevent me from hurrying him in an attempt to make him appear more active. I did not notice much in those two days of dressage, but I had appreciated that the judges marked an accurate but sparkless test very poorly. This was what I feared George would present – hence the jumping beforehand to try and return to him some of the zest he had shown in the spring.

The test did not seem brilliant, because George did not feel as supple and submissive as he might. Maybe my nerves had tensed me against him and prevented him from giving through his whole body. However, it must have looked better than it felt. His score headed the twelve British competitors and he lay third overall. Karl Schultz and Madrigal, Olympic bronze medallists, were over ten points ahead. A German lady rider was only a fraction of a point in front of George. Eyes and thoughts turned to the next day's decisive cross-country.

That evening the twelve British riders collected in the tented tackroom. With our new chef d'équipe, Tadzik Kopanski, and with Richard Meade and Dick Stillwell, we discussed together how best to attack the course and its thirty-three fences. It was a helpful hour for some. Others were reduced to tears when they discovered that they were the only ones who were intending to take a fence at a certain place while everyone else thought that particular route was crazy.

I was confident that I knew what I was going to try and ask George to do on the cross-country. Just before supper, several of us drove to the steeplechase course for one final walk round. A few days earlier, taking great pains to study this phase properly, Chris Collins, ex-champion amateur jump jockey, had kindly agreed to walk it with me as adviser. George was not a fluent jumper of steeplechase fences, and I had developed a time-consuming habit, at Burghley, of taking the wrong roped-off channel as I galloped round past the start to begin the second circuit.

The morning of cross-country day is not an easy one for the nerves. I do not like to walk the course, or parts of it, as all energy needs to be conserved for riding. George was not scheduled to start phase A until 3 p.m. There was a great deal of waiting to be done between breakfast and 3 o'clock. There are various remedies for these long waits. This time I did not go to my hotel bed until midnight, and, despite an optimistic 'daily' coming into my room twice during the next morning to make my bed, I did not wake up long enough to climb out until 11 o'clock. I dressed and wandered down to have some breakfast and read the papers. No breakfast, no papers. Instead, I ordered a lump of Cheddar cheese and, reckoning on the reviving powers of the beverage, a pot of tea, and took them back to my little bedroom.

I packed my cross-country clothes in a shoulder-bag and swung my crash-hat from the other arm. The queue of traffic outside the hotel was moving more slowly than I was walking as it trailed its way towards the great walls of Burghley Park. So much for my energy-saving routine. I was going to have to walk the mile down to the stables.

George was already plaited, although he still had three-quarters of an hour before he was due to be tacked up. He looked well enough, but drowsy and somewhat disinterested. I wondered if he felt any better than I did. I hoped so.

At exactly 3 o'clock, weighed out and suitably equipped, George and I started on the first leg of the speed and endurance phase of the 1977 European Championships. During the following one and a half hours I began to understand for the first time why this phase of the three-day event is so named.

George finished phase A sweating. It was not a hot day, but his sides heaved as he stood quietly at the start of the steeplechase. What a change from Be Fair whose nerves had always caused him to fidget about on his hind legs at the start. It crossed my mind to wonder if George was as healthy as he ought to be.

The first two fences felt good. George seemed safer and more sure of his jumping than he had done on the Badminton steeplechase. He was holding his neck and head in a fairly high position and jumping more off his hocks. He rounded the turn at the far end and gradually began to lose his style. His head and neck lowered, his rhythm altered as he lumbered onto his forehand. He felt a little tired already, and we had been barely one quarter of the way. He jumped the next three fences up the straight in such mediocre fashion that I wished there was not another entire circuit still to come. He began to lean on the left rein, heavier as he tired. He rounded the sharp turn at the top of the course and galloped, head bearing low, towards the roped-off channels, one of which formed the beginning of the second circuit. How I wished that it was the end. George felt tired. I was already beat. As we thundered down between the ropes with George leaning hard left, I must have shifted my weight, for in an instant he had moved a little to his left and tangled his galloping legs in the low-slung stringing of the channels. He tripped lower and lower with each stride, until I was sure that he would somersault. He stayed upright somehow and instead I shot over his head into the air and thudded sometime later to the ground. I clung to the reins as George galloped relentlessly on, dragging me along on my backside.

I remember being not in the slightest bit surprised. Somehow I had known for several hours that this day was going to be a disaster. Nothing had felt right. George hadn't. I hadn't. The atmosphere I had created for myself was all wrong. I bumped and bounced along the grass in between those pounding front feet, which never once touched me. The awfulness of the situation seemed in keeping with the past weeks. I told myself simply, 'You silly b . . . . , you knew you'd bog it but did you have to do it this early?'

Suddenly I realised that George seemed not to have noticed that I was no longer on his back but around his feet. I always thought he had a hard mouth, but I hadn't thought it could be insensitive enough to drag ten stone along without realising it. It did not seem that he was going to stop galloping and we were heading for a turn. Somehow I had to remind him of my whereabouts. I cannot remember why, but for some reason I had to cross on my bottom in front of his speeding legs in order to be in a better position to attract his attention and to stop him. Suddenly he seemed to hear 'Whoah, George, whoah', and felt a downward jag on the right-hand side of his mouth. He stopped quietly and quickly – apologetic at not having appreciated the situation earlier. He stood like a rock; 16.2 of big brown horse waiting to be remounted.

No one rushed to give me a leg-up. Any spectator that I could see was standing open-mouthed, transfixed by what they were watching and consequently rooted to the ground. With a huge heave which drained the last ounce of my flagging energy I half scrambled and half vaulted into the saddle. George set off again, head low, hocks strung well out behind, leaning hard to the left.

To this day I do not know how he jumped that last circuit of five fences. I could do nothing to help him. My battered old teddy would have coped better. When George was wrong for a fence he made no effort to shorten and adjust his stride but simply smashed through it. Galloping towards the open ditch, he was bearing so hard to port that I had to haul him back on course with both hands, lest he bypass the fence altogether.

I remember being certain that he could not remain standing up if he continued jumping like that. I was sure that he would be well over the time limit, and therefore had not bothered to look at my stop-watch since falling off. I felt sufficiently out of touch with things to entertain only one wish. I hoped that George would hurry up and fall and then I could be knocked unconscious and be able to sleep and sleep and sleep . . .

He almost missed the finish. Pulling hard left, George thundered towards the second-circuit channel once again, instead of through the finish. I stole a glance at my stop-watch as I flicked it back to zero for the start of phase C. It looked as if it said five minutes, but I did not believe my eyes. Five minutes was the time limit. I was certain that we must be outside it, and that we had knocked up a score of time penalties.

For the next eight kilometres I played alternately the rôles of nurse and persuader, as George struggled along the roads and tracks slowly, oh so slowly, recapturing some of the strength and energy that he had expended during our hectic steeplechase. In the back of my mind I wondered if he was a hundred per cent well, but there was nothing positive to prove this fractional suspicion.

We trotted into the Box; Tadzik ran up smiling. 'Did you know? You're OK. No time faults on the steeplechase.'

No wonder poor George had taken so long to recover on phase C. He must have completed that second circuit half a minute faster than he should have done, allowing for the time my fall had taken. Thankfully I handed him over to our well-organised team to wash him down and refresh him. Meanwhile I slumped into a striped plastic beach-chair and was briefed, quietly but firmly, by triple gold medallist Richard Meade as to how all thirty-three cross-country fences were jumping. I heard what he was saying, but I could barely take it in. The cross-country was of maximum length, nearly five miles, and over forty-five actual jumps to come. Even if George had the strength left, I knew that I had not and the more tired he was the more heavily he would lean on me. I begged not to be informed of the score position. I did not want to know that the British team was relying on us for a good clear round. George and I would do our best, but I was not at all confident that our best would be good enough. I left my collapsible chair and wandered to the tented ladies' loo, asking Lisa on the way to ensure the thickest possible layer of Vaseline was smeared down the front of all of George's legs. As I sat there I knew that there was nothing much left in me. Anything that happened now was entirely in the hands of my Maker. I asked His help.

To my surprise George sprang over the first two fences with feet to spare, revelling in the power of his own jump. He lowered himself neatly down the drop into the depths of the Leaf Pit below. The spontaneous bellow of the patriotic crowd sent us on our way with renewed courage and strength. He jumped hard left over the next fence and rattled both parts of the ensuing double. I yelled down his ear that he really must pick his feet up a bit better over the next twenty-nine. He listened and cooperated, though he became momentarily straddled as he lost his footing when bouncing out over the rails of the Half Coffin. He ate up the Irish Bank, the Trout Hatchery and the following four fences. He stood off an extra stride at the Troughs and I heard the gasp of the spectators. But George's limitless scope carried us out of trouble. I cursed myself for this near disaster as I had not gathered him together sufficiently before the fence. He took me over the next few fences, over the Hayrack, down past the Lake and past the tree that I had leaned against early the previous morning. He cantered up the Dairy Mound and popped over the Jubilee Tables – no trouble, because no serious collecting up was needed.

The first of the fences which I feared most was closing in on us. It was 3 foot 8 inches high and it was at the summit of the steep bank into Capability's Cutting. Unfortunately it was approached off a downhill turn. It was that turn which would be our problem. George would have preferred to canter straight on, continuing homewards. At the last moment he turned left-handed, answering my repeated demands, but he did not notice any collection aids. Only because he is the bold horse he is, was he able to stumble and prop over those rails and down the bank. Any normal horse, similarly uncollected and badly presented, would either have stopped or fallen.

Three fences later came the second of my three worries. Another sharp turn into a post and rails set on the far side away from the lip of a bank and ditch. Without my usual strength, I found it impossible to gather him together. Once again he crashed across it, legs everywhere. Once again he saved the day. As we cantered up the slope towards the last little strip of wood, I was glad that I had always agreed with Frank Weldon that men were preferable to women in teams as they coped better with stress and strains. I think I would have cried and flopped off then and there, I felt so weak, but for an English country gentleman who raised his shooting stick high in the air as George, head low and heavy, mouth dead, galloped by: 'Come on, England; come on, George!' he shouted in encouragement.

One more straightforward fence preceded the complications of the Double Coffin and my third worry. All I could do to prepare him for the Double Coffin was to turn his face into the crowd in an endeavour to slow him down. Using my voice to encourage him again I turned him to face the palisade on the brink of the bank at whose base there was a double of ditches, a stride up another bank followed by a palisade out. Once more all praise to that incredible horse.

102

He picked up his feet and leaped neatly over all four parts. The cheers of the spectators were deafening. George had earned it all and more. As for me, I have never felt less deserving of such support.

Thus George finished my least favourite speed and endurance test with only 5.4 time faults, putting the British team into a good lead and himself into second place individually, nine penalties behind Karl Schultz and Madrigal.

For the first time I failed to summon either the energy or the enthusiasm for phase E and did not attend the Burghley ball that evening. Alone in my little bedroom I felt a profound gratitude to my Maker. There was no doubt that He had been working overtime that Saturday afternoon.

Sleep was no problem. The fact that I was within a fence of a second European Championship did not excite me. It barely occurred to me. In spite of Madrigal's dicey show-jumping ability I thought that he would go clear. Karl Schultz had ridden an excellent cross-country round and deserved to win. I did not feel justified in lying second, let alone winning.

All Sunday morning, Oliver Plum, my cavalier spaniel and constant companion for seven years, was seen wandering pathetically around the car park of the George Hotel. I did not notice his absence all day. Fortunately, by lunch-time my mother had noticed and she performed the necessary rescue. My mind was functioning with even less speed than it was the day before. In church that morning I was twice left standing up on my own when the congregation was already on bended knee.

At Peter Scott-Dunn's private vet's inspection late the previous night, George had seemed none the worse for his exertions. After a good sleep he was perky and bright when we went for a gentle ride around the park in the morning. With his muscles suitably unstiffened he passed the official vet's inspection and went back to his stable for a little more rest until the Grand Parade at 2 o'clock.

He was a tired horse. I warmed him up after the parade as gently and progressively as possible. He did not give me the same feeling of lightness and elasticity as he had done five months earlier at Badminton. He felt old, as if he no longer loved every step he trod. I jumped only a few practice fences. He was not making any effort to jump well. Either he knocked the pole down or he skimmed across the top. Apart from putting on a sharper pair of spurs I did not know what to do with him to ensure that he jumped the vital clear round. But what I did know was that I must not continue practising. We walked up to the stadium area with only one thin shred of hope in our combined abilities to jump clear. George might sense the occasion and make the effort in the arena that he was unwilling to make outside it.

Lisa led George round. With his pale blue Union Jack emblazoned rug thrown over his saddle and loins, he looked man enough. But his head was low and his feet dragged a little across the centuries-old turf. I went over to the arena to watch Schultz and Madrigal jump. I felt that George had had enough. I could see no reason why he should not go into that arena and knock down five fences, as apparently he had done a few years earlier.

At all international team competitions, competitors jump on the final day in programme order, not in reverse order of placings. It so happened that George was last to go in the programme and now with all to play for, the tension in the arena noticeably mounted as time ran on.

Madrigal was jumping well. He had to jump a clear round to retain his tenuous lead and I found myself hoping that he would do this, so that the pressure would be off George and me. It wouldn't then matter quite so much if we knocked a few down, since there would have been no chance of an individual gold, and the British team already had several fences in hand.

The penultimate fence rattled to the ground. Madrigal

emerged with ten penalties. George and I had to clear twelve small fences to become European Champions . . . *only* twelve fences. It was twelve too many. I hung on to my shred of confidence, hoping that through his innate intelligence George would sense the importance of the event and would react accordingly.

Five minutes before we were due to jump I remounted and Dick Stillwell helped us with a few practice fences. George jumped idly. Dick made the fence very big. George hit it hard. He came round again and jumped it better. He felt laboured, but he had tried. We stopped jumping and walked slowly around the collecting ring. Dick came over and gave my backside a painful pinch and said, 'C'mon girl, what's up with you then? Will you please wake yourself up?' My mother had spotted the daze I was in and had mentioned it to Dick, knowing he would understand how best to cope with the situation.

Sioux and Horst Karsten were lying third. They cantered out of the arena with one fence on the floor. George walked towards the entrance. Dick delivered another nerve-awakening pinch; I smiled and we trotted into the arena.

Never had I been more grateful to the Great British public. They roared as George came in. Their enthusiasm and tension transmitted themselves instantly to him. He pricked his ears and threw out his toes as he floated in extended trot towards the Royal Box. We halted and saluted, and as we moved off into canter an extraordinary silence fell on the whole of the Burghley stadium.

How George jumped over the top of those twelve fences and not through the middle I do not know. Through his idleness and tiredness he might become careless if he met a fence 'right', so I encouraged him to come in very close to the first six. He had to perform a series of gymnastic feats to get himself out of trouble. But he knew. He was determined not to hit anything. Gradually, I relaxed a little and dared to ride him more 'forward', thereby making his task easier.

We squared up for the final fence, a red-brick wall. The hush was dramatic as several thousands must have held their breath. Earlier I had watched three out of six people knock a brick from the top of this wall. Would George flick one out too and lose everything . . . ?

I couldn't stop the new European Champion as he ran away around the arena. The noise of the ecstatic home crowd went to both our heads. He galloped on, round and round, my feeble pulls having no effect. But then they had not had much effect over the past three days, and yet George had still managed to clinch for Britain the European team title and to win for himself the individual gold medal. He was a brilliant horse. I thought how pleased my father would have been, and hoped that he had been watching from his new front-row seat in the skies.

The Burghley sponsors, Raleigh, gave both Elaine and me a bicycle. We cycled around in a daze for a while clutching a bottle of champagne between us. 'You don't breed them like George – they just happen,' was all she could say.

Maybe George was harbouring a touch of Killaire's virus or maybe he was becoming a little old. It did not really matter what the reason was. I knew I did not want to ask him the big question again. Despite me, he had given everything he had when he did not feel himself. Despite me, he had made history by winning both Badminton and Burghley in one year and by winning a second European championship for me. How could I ask him more?

Eleven

Killaire started serious work again five weeks before he found himself in an aeroplane bound for Boston. Once again the generosity of Neil Ayer, owner and organiser of Ledyard Three-Day Event, had invited and paid for a plane full of European horses and riders to fly out and compete against the Americans.

Killaire's superlative honesty was thoroughly tested at Ledyard. But it left me unenthusiastic about asking him to face a major three-day event again.

The cross-country was as big and questioning as any three-day event outside Badminton and the Olympics. The terrain was hilly but the going was not as hard as it could have been in early October. The temperature was not high but the atmosphere was rainy and close. Killaire would find the cross-country alone little problem if it were not preceded by two miles of steeplechase.

Unable to release my foot from the accelerator for one single stride if Killaire was not to lose valuable points on phase B, we managed to scramble past the finish flags without one second extra in hand. He recovered his breath quite quickly and I felt that he had plenty left in his tank for the cross-country. Exactly how much, I could have no idea.

Once again if he was to have any chance of a reasonably good time in the cross-country he would have to go as fast as his legs could carry him from start to finish.

He shot through the start and scurried across the well-covered ground to pop across the first fence. His head and neck adopted their habitual and uncomfortably low line after a further four fences. We nearly paid for this weakness as we dived over a fence, dropping vertically down onto a road similar to Capability's Cutting at Burghley. This time he very nearly did fall. He landed in an unbalanced heap in the bottom and pitched across the road on his nose heading for a staunch, unbending tree. Maybe he too saw similar visions of doing a headstand against the trunk, for at the last second he regained his balance and swerved to avoid it. Pulling his head up from below his ankles he pounded on. Five fences from home the course passed close to the finish for a second time. Killaire refused to believe that this time he had not finished. It was all I could do to keep him going over the final fences, two of which were the biggest and most difficult on the course.

The penultimate fence was a parallel of hedges in a ditch at the bottom of a steep hill. The ground was false and boggy in the valley and what little effort Killaire could make was sucked away by the take-off. He decided the best way to negotiate this green expanse was to bank it like the good Irish hunter he is. His front feet understandably disappeared down between the two hedges and resignedly I leant well back and prepared for a crash landing. 'What a wretched shame to have got this far only to fall,' I thought. Already I began to curse myself as I was sure I had not allowed for the sinking take-off and had not ridden at the fence sufficiently strongly. At that point Charles Cyzer broke his worry-beads as he watched in anguish. I do not know from where Killaire found the extra energy but he made a superhuman effort and, off air alone, propelled himself upwards to give his front feet time to disentangle themselves before his nose hit the ground on the far side. He survived. His powers of self-preservation are enormous but his heart is even bigger. He jumped the last fence and lest we galloped past the finish once again without stopping, he put the brakes on and refused to canter any further. We finished at trot. He had given everything he had and it left me with an uncomfortable and unsatisfactory feeling.

Except for Ellie May I had only ridden class horses in big events and they rarely finished a cross-country course tired. Killaire would always have to be pushed and shoved along and he was always going to finish tired. He was simply not cut out to be an event horse and it seemed unkind to make him try so hard.

His time faults on the cross-country were not the lowest, they never will be, but he was only fifteen seconds away from the target and earned himself fourth place. Charles and Annie were delighted. We could enjoy even more the fantastic parties that the Americans were constantly throwing, in our relief at Killaire's safe homecoming.

He felt full of fun the next day despite his efforts on the cross-country. By virtue of another of his self-styled clear rounds and because poor Bruce Davidson knocked one down with Irish Cap, Killaire moved into third place. Mike Plumb, one of the greatest three-day event riders of all time, at last earned just reward for his endeavours. On the beautiful ex-Australian horse, Laurenson, he won. On the American thoroughbred, Better and Better, he was second.

The weekend before Ledyard I had ridden Gossip at Knowlton One-Day Event, near Canterbury, to warm him up for Boekelo in two weeks' time. The intervening weekend was spent at Ledyard. Lisa was with Killaire in the United States and little Jo came back to take Gossip once again to Holland, where, fresh from Boston, I met them.

It was a hectic month. I thought I was enjoying it but there was not time to turn round and make sure. The gear-box inside my head had switched over to automatic several weeks before. It became stuck until the end of the season in this auspicious slot. Gossip sped round Boekelo, the only horse inside the time, and was beaten into second place by his Luhmühlen vanquisher, the fourteen-year-old German horse, Sioux, and Horst Karsten.

1977, an unprecedented year, drew to a close. The double sevens indicated the year of the lucky doubles. It was Lisa's first year with me and she had already become a major asset. She was a pillar of support during a time when, for me, eventing had lost most of its spark and its fun. Her Christmas present was a cigarette lighter which bore her name, the year, and

GEORGE 1st 1st
VILLAGE GOSSIP 2nd 2nd
KILLAIRE 3rd 3rd

Before that Christmas she barely smoked.

A month after Ledyard a huge advertisement appeared in the *Horse and Hound*. Killaire was for sale. Charles realised that Killaire would always be a second-string horse due to his lack of speed. After much discussion with myself and others he decided to put him on the market and sell him if there was a sufficiently good offer.

OUTSTANDING
INTERNATIONAL EVENT HORSE

KILLAIRE

(9 yrs by Carnatic, 16 hands 3in)

2nd BURGHLEY (1976)

3rd BADMINTON (1977)

3rd LEDYARD (1977)

ELIGIBLE WORLD AND OLYMPICS
SOUND

Twelve

It is impossible to write this book without referring briefly to the sponsorship without which it could not have been completed.

At the beginning of 1978 one of our leading three-day event riders claimed that too many people in the horse world were trying to have their cake and eat it. He stated that people were claiming that they could not afford to refuse a big offer for their horse. 'What do they want?' he queried. 'Either they want the money or they want to ride for England. But they are trying to have the money and ride for England.'

They are, he is right. Sadly the standard is such that it is now virtually impossible to ride for England without having the money as well.

Today, in order to attain world standard in any sport, many hours must be spent in dedicated training. In our materialistic world time means money. This seems to be borne out by the fact that in three-day eventing no new young talent has tunnelled its way to the top for eight years. I believe that my generation was possibly the last that could reach the top on one horse, an average-size family income and bounteous good fortune.

My father worked until he was seventy-three in order to maintain Appleshaw and my full-time horse pursuits. Once his income ceased we were faced with the inevitable decision: either I gave up competing or I found a commercial sponsor who would underwrite the bills. Generous owners' livery fees were no longer enough to keep the show on the road.

Appleshaw and her family are indebted to Brian Giles, sports correspondent to the *Daily Mail*. He swung the pendulum into action by writing an article shortly after George won Burghley entitled 'Lucinda's call for sponsors'. The television followed this up with an interview. Humiliating as it was, a mercy plea was the only viable alternative.

The telephone started to ring, and several nerve-racking months later came the best Valentine of my life. February 14th, 1978 was the day on which Overseas Containers Limited, one of the largest container shipping lines in the world, gave a party for the press to announce their financial support of my horse endeavours through to the Moscow Olympics. A specified annual budget to cover the horses' expenses was announced and a sum was laid aside to buy one new horse.

A small posse of people had involved themselves in much hard work, some of them sticking their necks out and risking their reputations, solely in order to enable Miss P.-P. to continue her riding. I was overwhelmingly grateful but deep down I wondered if I was worth all their trouble. I began to wonder whether or not I could justify such support.

I had fallen on my feet yet again. It seemed our problems, at least for the next three years, were over. Materialistically they were. Mentally they were just beginning.

The responsibility that sports sponsorship must entail had always made me shudder. I am now sure that if the recipient is too young he or she could be razed by its effect rather than fortified.

I was lucky. No chairman, or board, could possibly be more friendly or more fun than OCL's. From the beginning their attitude was 'We only want to help so that she can continue without worry.'

Nevertheless a great deal of money was being spent and it must be justified.

Uncertainty and indecision were rife as I wondered how

to construct the promised string of top-class event horses. Three years was too short a time to do this, but I must make an attempt.

Over the years several young horses of varying ages had collected at Appleshaw and were now ready and waiting to have time and money spent on them. In my inexperience and with only modest sums to hand they came in all shapes and sizes and within a year only two proved to be worth keeping on: Resolution Bay and Botany Bay (Be Brave).

William Micklem had a flash of ingenuity and suggested that his brother, Charlie, an able ex-National Hunt jockey, should come to Appleshaw to be co-jockey. He came as second jockey but beat me too often to remain under that title.

It takes between three and five years and an overdose of luck to take a young horse through to the top. Apart from Gossip there were no top-class horses to offer OCL and therefore no publicity to benefit them.

As anyone who has tried will know, top horses are hard to come by and there was little question of going out and buying one. They have to be made, through years of patience and work.

Killaire had not been sold and was returning for Badminton. It was thrilling to have him back because he was such a very special person. The prospect of pursuing him around another three-day event was less thrilling.

I still felt strongly that it was wrong to ask George to do any more for me and therefore he was not returning to Appleshaw. As I struggled to find an understanding with Gossip, I began to miss George more and more. Frequently during that spring I questioned the decision I had made after Burghley.

On the unpredictable Village Gossip, therefore, hinged the success or failure of OCL's sponsorship in this first vital year.

Thirteen

If the measure of a good rider is repeated success on a number of different horses then I suppose I should have qualified by 1978. But my chief ambition had always been to be able to ride any horse. Once someone can climb on anything and produce the best from that horse immediately, he can rightfully claim to be an artist. My principal objective is to be able one day to rely on the imperishable quality of skill and not the transient quality of luck.

It remained blatantly clear to me that I was no artist. With this strongly in mind I went to America during the winter of 1977 to spend a few weeks with two genuine artists in their own right: Bert de Nemethy, the United States' Hungarian show-jumping coach, and Jack Le Goff, the United States' French three-day event coach. As well as being another fascinating experience, it served principally to confirm once again that I was still a rainbow's length from my goal.

The 1978 spring season approached and for the first time I did not want to meet it. The new pressures of sponsorship should have formed a challenge that I was keen to attack. Instead, I wanted to bolt.

I was twenty-four and still spending my whole life and a great deal of other people's time and money on one comparatively futile object. Myself. It was high time that a more worthy objective was found.

Killaire had not been himself during the last month before Badminton. His coat did not gleam and his blood count showed that he was still anaemic, a condition he sometimes suffered in mid-winter. He had been given a few days off, as we suspected he had tweaked a tendon cantering on the hills, when he contracted a form of mud-fever. This left one front leg a similar size to the school cook's. Whatever we did to it the filling would not go down. It became impossible to work him and the inflammation made it equally impossible to calculate how seriously he had strained his tendon. He was withdrawn from Badminton and taken home to Sussex for a long summer convalescence.

While walking the Badminton cross-country course in 1978, the enormity of the obstacles and the complexity of their problems struck me with as much force as they had done in 1972, Be Fair's and my first year. Boekelo and Luhmühlen were incomparable to what now faced Gossip. Would he do it? Strong doubts existed. We understood each other a little better than we used to. Two weeks before, at Rushall, I had finally dared to release the pressure on the reins and allowed him to go flat out into his fences. In consequence he gave me his safest and most exhilarating ride and won the advanced class. Our mutual confidence had taken a big step forward that spring but I did not fully trust him and, likewise, he did not fully trust either me or the fences. Frequently he would spook like a green horse at what he had to jump, but so far he had only refused if checked too close in front of a fence. Except for crumpling on landing during his first Boekelo, he had never fallen. Might Badminton not be the test which tipped the balance?

On paper he was ready for the challenge. He had done Tidworth three times, Bramham, Burghley and Luhmühlen once, and Boekelo twice. In reality I had absolutely no idea if his attitude would stand the test of Badminton.

The fun had melted from this particular conquest. In its place an emptiness hardened. I failed to understand it, but to my horror it eventually reduced me to tears as I dragged my feet round the cross-country course for the third and final time. After six years of loving every element of Badminton and every emotion which it inspired, suddenly and unaccountably this year there was no joy, no uplifted heart.

I was not loving what I was doing any more, in fact I was almost hating it. Without inspiration and laden with new pressures I could see no other way to go but downhill fast, into the depths of despair. To add to the unease, as Gossip now belonged to my principal owners OCL, he was destined to be ridden first and was to start Number 1 on the cross-country. Killaire would have been my second ride.

I was too screwed up to say much to anyone except to tell the press that it definitely was not my turn this year. 'It will not happen again. No . . . so please go away and leave me alone.'

Mummy has antennae that before now have sensed situations at the critical moment. A note had been slipped under my bedroom door by the time I awoke on cross-country morning.

'What happens today is in the hands of your Maker. No one expects Gossip to do any good. He is an unknown quantity at this level; so don't worry, just go out there and feel it's the two of you against Frank Weldon and his course. And don't forget you do do it for *fun*.' To combat my negative mood of the present she had sensed the necessity of creating some aggression. Several pounds' weight lifted from my head – I had never thought of it as a duel between ourselves and the course-builder. And hell, why did I need so much reminding these days? Was that not exactly why I did do it, for a challenge, for *fun*?

Finding that he had nothing to fight and was free to gallop as fast as he liked around the course and into the fences Gossip jumped nearly every single fence with the ease, neatness and élan of a star. I did not believe that he would be able to keep up such a pace for four and a half miles, but he finished the course as keenly as he had begun. Most of my arrangements had to be made by altering my weight and balance on his back and not by pulling or fighting with his mouth. He was forty-five seconds inside the time limit and it is the only time that I have finished riding the cross-country at Badminton without feeling tired myself – a measure of how still I had to sit and how little riding Gossip permitted.

It was only when the cross-country was over and I felt completely different that my consciousness discovered what my sub-conscious had always known. It had been crucially important to christen OCL's first major involvement in three-day eventing with success and not disaster.

A clear round in the show-jumping, still employing our new-found fast but fluent style, left Gossip runner up to Warrior and Jane Holderness-Roddam.

The OCL tent at Badminton swelled with excitement. The drinks and good cheer flowed.

Those unfortunates who ride for companies which do bring pressure to bear must be made of steel. The teething problems of an unpressurised sponsorship were nearly too much for me.

Equally admirable are those who manage on their own without the vital stamp of support which is accorded me by my remarkable family and those about me.

'Three parts of success lies in the mind, one part in inspiration.'

Throughout the rest of 1978 I learned to live, to ride and to compete with neither inspiration nor urge. Nothing outstanding occurred in competitions and I knew it could not as there was no fire and no ardour.

Fourteen

Killaire flew with Gossip and the British team to Lexington, Kentucky. Charles had kindly agreed to allow his horse to go to the World Championships as team reserve.

Killaire enjoyed himself immensely and was probably the only horse in the entire barn (all ten nations were stabled under one roof) who did enjoy the 1978 championships. He became the barn favourite, charming everyone with his consistent smiles. After the close of declarations the day before the event Killaire ceased to do serious work but was taken out for a fun ride every day; more than that he did not have to do. Diana Lithgow, Colonel Bill's daughter, took him for a ride along the edge of the course the morning after the cross-country. When he saw the dreaded Serpent fence he suddenly shot off towards it. It took Diana all her strength to prevent him jumping it. He even had the fun of the final parade before the show-jumping as Gossip was too tired after his cross-country day's exertions to be brought out to jump the following day. Later, back in England, I gathered that the *real* reason why Village Gossip had not show-jumped was because 'she had been so upset at being placed only eleventh'.

We did not deserve to be any nearer the World Championship. No partnership deserves to win if it cannot work in complete unison. If it cannot, for instance, choose its pace to suit the circumstances. Gossip fell at the infamous Serpent, seven fences from home. Until then he had maintained his Badminton style and speed, but it was not 55°F of English spring weather, instead it was 90°F and 95 per cent of mid-American humidity. We fell because Gossip was exhausted, a state which neither of us had thought could possibly overtake him.

His staggering courage and what remained of his killer instinct picked him up from the murky water and took him to the end of the course, but only just.

For the first time I wished that I was not in the British team as I coaxed, encouraged and actually beat him over the last seven fences. Had we been competing as individuals and not in Number 1 position for the team I would not have asked Gossip to continue. To find myself in this somewhat ruthless rôle made me question seriously the justification of having a World-class *team* competition when three-day eventing is essentially an individual sport. Four people can still ride for their country but each without the added dimension of pressure produced by the knowledge that three others are relying on their performance for a team result. Most other Olympic sports involve a team of individuals representing their country; why should three-day eventing differ?

There may still be some roundheads who would push their horses too hard, but without a team to use as their excuse they would have no shield. Competitors do not reach international level if they find it easy to make the decision to pull out. Being a member of a team, I believe, tips the balance in the moment of decision away from the right judgement.

Watching one courageous horse after another struggle through the finish at Lexington split any thread of glamour that three-day eventing still wove through me. If that was my sport at top level then I was in the wrong one. Many others, I think, felt likewise.

Apart from Dauntsey, where he registered his first win on British soil, and the Midland Bank Championships at Locko, where he was fifth, Killaire had only one other competition in 1978, the Dutch National Championships in

Boekelo. He had an easy year, giving his slightly strained tendon and his impaired health plenty of time to recover.

Boekelo held no hardships for Killaire. He was third after an improved dressage but took advantage of his passive, 'Kentucky-fried-jockey' and recorded time faults on both the steeplechase and the cross-country. A careless mistake in the show-jumping relegated us to fifth place.

Fifteen

OCL had produced sponsorship in order to ensure that my path to the Olympics should be as clear as possible. Consequently it was imperative that we should have a horse of the right standard and age for 1980. Even if our young horses proved to be of a high enough standard they would not be ready for Olympic competition by then. George had retired and Killaire must be a doubtful starter in two years' time. Anyhow neither of them belonged to OCL. All OCL's Olympic eggs were therefore in one basket, Village Gossip. By 1980 he would be twelve and, tough as he might be, he had galloped flat out around ten three-day events in five years. It was irresponsible and unrealistic to expect him to maintain sufficient working order for a further two years. A reserve egg must be fostered but *where* were they laid? All year I had been searching for an intermediate standard horse. I hoped to find one that was half way up the ladder and could possibly be trained on during the next two years, to Olympic standard. It quickly became apparent that a large number of others were looking for the same type of horse. It also quickly became apparent that such animals rarely exist. It seemed that if anyone was willing to sell a horse that had reached the half-way stage in its career, either there was something wrong with it or it was for sale at a ridiculously high price, which only foreigners could afford.

Eventually, almost by accident I bought a horse at the end of the World Championships in the USA. The Kiwis had to sell their horses as they could not afford to fly them home to New Zealand. This particular one, although he had finished second from bottom, had performed very creditably. Buying top-class horses in order to continue top-class eventing was furthest from my mind following Lexington's unappetising example of these summits. It was solely the interest of Lady Hugh Russell that aroused me from my indifference and made me look twice at this little white bundle of power with the temperament of a child's pony.

Thus, ultimately, a new face joined the Appleshaw winter holiday-resort at the end of 1978. A white one. His name, Mairangi Bay alias Bandolier. His breeding and origin, a half Arab pony from New Zealand.

The relief of having at least made an attempt to secure an insurance policy for OCL's Moscow bid combined with a stimulating break of two horseless months, save for a momentous day's hunting with dear George in Yorkshire, recharged the batteries. I could not wait to welcome in 1979.

Killaire returned to Appleshaw barely a month before Badminton. None of us had seen him in such fine fettle before. Charles had a good system working for him at his home, where head girl Gabrielle, helped by Frances, looked after and broke valuable colts and fillies as well as building up Killaire during the all-important first two months of his training. His big bright eyes gleamed expectantly. His kindly but boyish cheek was in abundance.

While schooling he would pretend that he was working from behind and carrying himself properly. When eventually I realised his con and attempted to make him work, his tail flew round like a windmill as he produced little bunny-bucks in rebellion. He was well again and he was moving better and more openly than in previous years.

He roared out of control around the dressage, the show-jumping and the cross-country at Rushall, his only preparatory one-day event, where he recorded an identical cross-country time to that of Village Gossip and was placed third.

Gossip's Rushall performance was reasonable but it

aroused dormant post-Lexington suspicions. He had not run away as fast as usual between fences and he had bungled one fence trying to refuse it. I had feared that Lexington would leave its mark and when a brief trickle of blood ran from his nose at the end of the cross-country I wondered how serious a mark it would prove to be. Only time would tell.

1979, we had felt, would be Gossip's year. Like Killaire he was eleven years old, a prime age for many event horses. If our partnership should ever be sealed, I felt it would have to happen this year. After Rushall it seemed evident that this could no longer be expected. Apart from the worry that he may not want to do the cross-country any more, communications in the dressage, which had been linking up favourably during the winter, had broken down once again. The evening after Rushall I mused at my fortune, in the circumstances, to still have the ride on Killaire.

During January he had come extremely close to being sold in order that Richard Meade could be mounted.

Vin Jones had generously lent his Bleak Hills to Richard for the previous year's Badminton and Lexington. Understandably he was reluctant to be grounded for a further year and would only release Bleak Hills to Richard if a substitute Badminton horse could be found for himself. With both Gossip and Mairangi Bay already in our stable, Killaire seemed the obvious answer.

I was sure that Killaire had seen his golden days as a nine-year-old when he was third at both Badminton and Ledyard and that he could not be expected to reproduce such efforts again. I adored him but, leaving emotions aside, it seemed only fair to support the move to procure a ride for triple gold medallist Richard.

The sale fell through because of a slight doubt over the presence of an old and small injury high up on Killaire's near-fore leg. His return to Appleshaw was a delight.

Five American riders and their horses arrived at Wylye in

mid-March to launch an attack on Badminton six weeks later. Neither dual World Champion, Bruce Davidson, nor Mike Plumb, was among them. Both their horses needed longer to recover after Lexington. Jimmy Wofford did come, however, with the ex-English horse Carawich who had completed Lexington with only one fall and been placed tenth. It was because of Jimmy that Killaire arrived at Badminton as fit as he did and yet still as keen as when he had begun his training.

It is often difficult to hold a non-blood horse's interest during the fairly monotonous fitness work leading up to a three-day horse trials. Killaire is no exception. A horse's mental welfare is as important if not more so than his physical fitness, particularly if he is not a hot-blooded horse. If he is ground into a bored pulp before he arrives at a three-day event he may lose the necessary spirit which will carry him over the last dozen cross-country fences where a non-blood horse will almost certainly be tiring if he has gone fast. Jimmy advised me on a plan of how to make him fitter with less boring and repetitious work (see Appendix 1).

The spring of 1979 undoubtedly helped as the continuous rain enabled Killaire to do all his work on the hills, which never became too firm. He still hates hard ground and is never allowed to work on it.

Gossip was pursuing a more normal programme of inter-val training. It was the first time in one and a half years that he had been worked normally. Eighteen months ago he had struck into himself while doing slow canter work. He would not canter slowly and fought me, like a self-willed salmon on a hook, for his freedom. Since then, rather than risk breaking him down he was made fit by trotting him up and down hills. He is a wiry, hot-blooded, tough little thorough-bred and this it seemed was enough, as he had produced the fastest rounds at Luhmühlen, Boekelo, Badminton and Lexington (despite a fall). However, this time I wanted to be certain that he would not feel a second's tiredness at

17. 'How could I ask him more?' (*Chris Smith*)

18a. Killaire's head and neck in habitual low line . . .

18b. . . . but he could still produce a magnificent leap. Ledyard, 1977. (*Anne Holden*)

19. Killaire gazes knowingly into the distant oaks
of Badminton Park. 1979. (*Thomas Noel*)

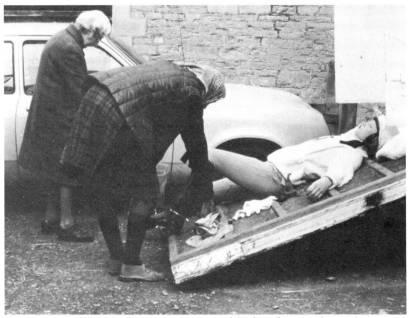

20a. Gossip's disappointing round had undermined any desire to attack. Mummy and Nanny in attendance. Badminton, 1979. (*Thomas Noel*)

20b. Our one nasty moment. Killaire, the Footbridge, Badminton, 1979. (*Hugh Neill*)

21. Killaire listens and obeys my checks . . .
and with three neat bounces takes us safely through the Dog
Kennel. Badminton, 1979. (*Bob Langrish*)

22. For Charles Cyzer it was more than deserved.
(*From left to right*: H. M. the Queen, the Duke of Beaufort,
H. R. H. the Duke of Edinburgh, Charles Cyzer
and Lt. Col. Frank Weldon.) (*Peter Harding*)

23. Killaire, lap of honour, Badminton, 1979.
Next stop, Luhmühlen and the European Championships.
(*Findlay Davidson*)

24. Be Fair, after winning the European Championships
in Luhmühlen, 1975. His hunting injury
filled me with remorse. He had done so much for me –
in fact he had given me a life.
(*Jürgen Gebhardt, Bild Zeitung*)

Badminton, lest he should remember the feeling from Kentucky and lose heart. Eating much spinach and flexing aching biceps I sat it out. Rarely was I able to stand up in my stirrups as Gossip, interpreting this as the signal for full speed ahead, would battle even more fiercely for his freedom.

Brand's Hatch is very near the Cyzers' home. I did not dare tell Killaire's owner that his jockey was destined to take part in a twelve-lap race around this Grand Prix circuit on Easter Sunday, four days before riding his horse in the most important three-day event in the calendar.

Unexpectedly, the practice sessions at Brand's Hatch were almost identical to walking a cross-country course – the objective of both was to discover and learn the safest and most economical line.

Racing against eleven other sportsmen and women in 1300 saloons, half-passing at full throttle around hair-pin bends, was a fine preparation for the coming weekend. Shot-putter and panda-car driver Geoff Capes was unbeatable. Astonishingly I enjoyed the unexpected delight of tailing him past the black and white chequered flag. Was the outcome a good omen for Badminton? Inspiration soared as spirits received an unforeseen injection of positive thinking.

Armed with the two diverse characters, found in Village Gossip and Killaire, Lisa, her new apprentice Liz and I drove to Badminton. Mummy, Simon, my sister Karol, her husband and family arrived later in the week, and Nanny, now sufficiently recovered from her heart attack to resume her twice-yearly visits to Appleshaw, came with them.

If Gossip performed an average dressage test and *if* he was all right after Lexington to do the cross-country in his own inimitable style he had a good chance of being well placed. Killaire had as good a chance as ever of being third. I often thought how much he deserved to win but I knew that even his very best could not be quite good enough to win the 'Big B'.

Gossip was first to go again as he was the best horse. Killaire, as Number 69, was near the end. After a reasonably controlled test, certainly the best that Gossip and I had done together, we received a poor mark. It was becoming increasingly depressing that his reputation stalked like a spectre into the arena well before he did. Jimmy Wofford made a filthy and extremely funny joke referring to the ungenerous marks later that day. It made me laugh so much that it set me back on a positive train of thought for Killaire's dressage the following day.

Jimmy can be held greatly responsible for the superlative performance that Killaire produced in the dressage arena the next afternoon. Jimmy and Carawich were leaving the arena as we entered it. Beforehand he had promised to tell me a joke to settle my nerves as we passed each other.

I thought he had forgotten for he smiled and rode past. It was all part of his plan to take my attention off the forthcoming test. At the last second he turned in his saddle and called out, 'Hey! What did the monkey say when the train ran over his tail?'

I thought for a little while. 'I don't know, what did he say?'

'It won't be long now.' Jimmy walked on.

Working around the outside of the arena boards awaiting the signal to start the dressage test is normally a tense time. This time it was not and I still had the giggles when Killaire cantered dead straight up the centre line and halted, four square, to bow to the three judges. I'm not sure if it was the entry or the giggles that earned us a nine and two eights out of ten for the first movement. The marks remained high throughout the ten-minute test.

It was one of the few tests that I have ridden as positively as if I had been schooling at home. Killaire responded to the best of his short-striding ability. He stood second, a point behind Judy Bradwell and Castlewellan, at the end of the dressage. Killaire's staggering improvement, considering he has no natural paces, is due principally to David Hunt, to Ernst Bachinger and to Brigid Maxwell. Since her return to England a year ago, having spent five years with Herbert Rehbein, Brigid has helped Charlie and me tremendously with our horses.

Killaire stood in the collecting ring after his dressage with his head held unusually high. Ears pricked, he was lost in his imagination as he gazed into the distant oaks of the Park. Mummy caught his look. She had seen it before on Be Fair, at some point during his great Badminton triumph. It was a proud, knowing look. I noticed it too, but attached little importance to it. Killaire might do well but he was simply not cut out to win.

For the eighth consecutive year, on the eve of the cross-country I found Dick Stillwell to hoover any last-minute advice he might have to offer. The trust I have in him usually manages to clear up at least one, if not all of two or three, final indecisions.

Gossip did not make his usual fast time around the steeplechase and was only seven seconds inside the limit. He was not quite himself but he would die before he stopped galloping, and so, yet again, he was without time faults on the cross-country, despite a refusal that in no way was his fault. He lacked lustre, however, and he jumped without joy. It seemed his body no longer possessed the strength of his mind. The last few drop fences found him tumbling vertically onto his nose and knees. He did not fall over but he should have done.

Depressed and embittered at the thought that the World Championships had in fact taken its toll of Gossip I felt in no mood to kick Killaire round in order that he should clutch on to every point that he could.

The ground crew had work on their hands. They reminded the jockey that it *was* possible for Killaire to make the time. 'Don't forget Ledyard. He can do it, and he is really well and fit – but you have to push *every* stride.'

It took the expected amount of encouragement for Killaire to rumble through the finish of phase B clocking exactly five minutes. One second slower and we would have incurred penalties.

Mummy, Simon and Lisa had sensed the situation. They realised that Gossip's disappointing round had upset me and undermined my desire to attack; they knew that I would have little enthusiasm remaining with which to animate Killaire.

By the time Killaire and I rode into the Box at the finish of phase C, my spirits had sunk even lower. There was tremendous pressure for Killaire to do well. It was expected. Yet I did not feel sufficiently inspired after Gossip's round to do as much about it as I knew I should. Already I felt tired, a sure sign of how much riding Gossip had needed – for the first time.

My mother was at a loss as to how to galvanise me. Suddenly there was a shout from ground level behind the chestnut paling which enclosed the Box. It was Pat. Despite having a bus load of handicapped children to care for she had sensed that things were not right in my area. She could not force her way through the ten-deep crowd which surrounded the Box, so she crawled through their legs on hands and knees. Kneeling behind the fence she grabbed me by the hand and said something. I do not know what it was but it was enough to send a spark off the flint.

Killaire and I stood at the start of the cross-country; Charles Cyzer was nowhere to be seen.

'Don't forget his fantastic time at Ledyard,' smiled Lisa. 'He *can* do it.'

At the fifty-ninth second the spark that flew off the flint lit the tinder. She was right, he *could* do it. Castlewellan had fallen, and Richard Walker and Special Constable, and Jane Starkey and Topper Too, both close behind after the dressage, had dropped back. Killaire had a chance. I owed it to him, to Charles, to everyone connected with him, to endeavour to translate that chance into fact.

There is one nasty moment in nearly every great ride. We did not escape ours – at the Footbridge. It took skilful tucking up of his legs and all his aptitude to extricate himself from an odds-on fall as he slipped down the take-off bank and hit the Footbridge handrail with his forearms. Once again as in Ledyard he propelled himself upwards off air alone and landed intact on the far bank.

He listened and obeyed my checks as he sat on his hocks in front of every fence that required it. He was going like a class horse, no longer with his own headlong scuttle. Every stride had to be asked for but every stride was given with unaccustomed freedom. It was hardly credible that this was the same Killaire as the horse at Burghley in 1976.

He still took some inadvisable risks with anything green, either by banking it, or taking it by the roots. If he is not very careful, one day he will take one chance too many over a brush fence.

Killaire took the lead with less than a show-jump in hand over Monacle and Sue Hatherly, who had produced the type of class performance that makes the mouth water. I would have laid any amount of money against Killaire leading at the end of the cross-country day at Badminton. I had had my turn of winning and it felt unrealistic to expect that luck could produce a fourth Badminton win. I did not feel that I deserved it, but I did feel very strongly that if Killaire had managed to lead after the cross-country, then he at least thoroughly deserved the final accolade.

Gossip show-jumped extremely well. We enjoyed our show-jumping together now and clean happy rounds were no longer infrequent. There were only three clear rounds by the time Killaire's turn came and even Gossip had had a fence down, although he maintained his seventh place. One of those clears was Monacle. Killaire could not afford even one mistake.

Fearing he would pitch onto his forehand when he

started on the course I wanted him to hit a fence outside so the memory still stung his legs and reminded him to keep them tucked away when he went into the arena. Dick Stillwell did his best to make Killaire hit a fence out in the practice area but he would not. He was trying.

The tension of jumping in reverse order of merit does not lessen with familiarity. Dick produced his usual magic and managed to prevent the fan belt in my mind from snapping.

'You can't do it alone,' Pat whispered from the gate to the collecting ring as we rode into the arena. The huge crowd was still applauding Monacle's clear. Silence fell, a similar silence to that which had fallen on George at Burghley in 1977. Killaire stood four square to the Queen. I bowed. We turned and cantered away awaiting the bell. The silence was broken by the commentator. Very rarely do I hear what is said over the air but I picked up every word of it that time. '. . . at present in the lead . . . she needs a clear round to make a record-breaking fourth win. One fence down will put them behind Sue Hatherly and Monacle.' 'Oh do shut up,' I thought – I was trying to dispel such thoughts. There was a moment when I did not know how I was going to keep my cool and a low note of panic sounded deep down. Then I knew what Pat had meant: 'you are not alone.'

A calm seized me; something inside said, 'Come on, it's not the end of the world if you knock one down – you have only lost a competition. Get on through those start flags, stop hanging about, and start riding.' Killaire touched the fifth fence and I growled down his ear. I do not think he has ever before jumped so balanced and accurately as he did that day. The penultimate fence was the only one that we approached on completely the wrong stride. We chose to stand off and he did not flatten as a horse so often will. The last fence was a treble; many had knocked one part or the other. The best I could do was keep him in balance for the first part and then start praying even harder.

130

Killaire's middle name is Try. He landed clear and he won.

It still does not seem possible that one person should be granted, on four separate occasions, the humble ecstasy of harmony and communication with four highly couraged horses during the greatest three days of each of their lives.

From Killaire's angle this was life at its fairest. Victory was appropriate reward for sheer application. For Charles, his owner, it was a reward for the patience he had shown over the past two years while his horse had continuously played best man at my wedding.

Many fellow competitors were genuinely delighted for Killaire. His generous honesty shone through his lack of natural ability as brightly as his wide, dark eyes gleamed.

For the fourth consecutive week Britain's Number One in the pop charts was 'Bright Eyes'. It boomed from the horsebox radio as the champion and the seventh best were loaded, very much later that afternoon, to return home to Appleshaw. How any of us drove home without an accident I do not know.

Champagne magnanimously and liberally supplied to family and all about by Charles was running from our ears. OCL had become an extension of the family in the last year and they rejoiced alongside Charles. Their horse may not have won but they knew that without their support their jockey could not have won either.

During Badminton Be Fair was staying at his beloved Burley-on-the-Hill in order that Joss Hanbury could take him in a team cross-country race. George was spending the weekend similarly occupied with the Strakers in Yorkshire. I sent them both a silent thank you. Wide Awake received one too – probably the most strangely sensitive of the four, he formed the link between the dream co-existence of Be Fair and me and the reality of riding those that followed him. Wide Awake was responsible for teaching me the necessity to dig down and try to learn how to adjust to different horses.

Both Be Fair and George sent the new Badminton champion a telegram as he drew the fourth and final side, thereby closing an unbelievable square.

Napoleon Bonaparte would only choose lucky people to be his generals. Had I been around 170 years ago I think I would have found a job.

Epilogue

It was tempting Fate to finish this story with a happy ending. Apart from one deviation westwards in the spring of 1977, Killaire's ascent to the horse trials pinnacle was a direct northward climb.

At Badminton in 1979 we thought Killaire had reached his highest possible level of performance. Five months later during the European Championships, held once again at 'Be Fair's Luhmühlen', he soared on upwards. Producing an even better dressage he sped around the steeplechase in a personal best time, twelve seconds inside the limit and without the usual persistent encouragement from his jockey. Of his own intelligent accord he saved every yard of ground that he could by hugging the turning-flags so tightly that where they were positioned a few feet inside the grass track on the heathland Killaire would shoot round the turn on the heather.

He attacked the cross-country as if he meant, in one attempt, to blow out all the candles on his birthday-cake. For the first time I loved every minute of his round until the inevitable last few fences, when, like most of those before him, he tired in the heat of the day. He had made nearly fifty individual efforts over fences on a course that stretched the rules as well as the horses with the exorbitant number of combination fences it contained. Even on Be Fair I do not think that I had felt so completely confident all the way round a cross-country, so certain was I that Killaire would not hint at a mistake. He neither hit a fence nor stumbled on a landing and he finished with the fourth fastest time of the day. The vet recorded his pulse as the lowest of all the finishers in the event: 114 beats per minute.

Scoring the best in his team, Killaire pulled Great Britain into a virtually unassailable lead. He himself was tucked neatly behind the Dane Nils Haagensen on Monaco and the British individual rider Rachel Bayliss on Gurgle the Greek, within one show-jumping mistake of them and the Individual European Championship.

For one and a half hours it seemed too good to be true. Thus it proved to be.

That courageous and sensitive horse had tried maybe too hard. By the evening he was unaccountably lame on his off-fore leg. Was it foot? Was it tendon? Was it torn muscles higher up? None of us could tell. Everything was treated accordingly that night and with little hope we waited to see if a miracle would render him sound the following morning. If he was not sound he would not run which would mean the team would lose its winning position to the Irish. However, no prize merits such ill-reward to a horse as patching him up to jump if he is not fit do so.

At exactly the moment that Killaire was destined to have show-jumped on the third day the skies turned a gun-metal grey. A sudden fierce, swirling wind arose sending decorative spruce trees scrambling across the arena as cardboard hamburger containers leapt out of their litter bins and bobbed across the sandy ground.

The storm broke loose over the prize-giving ceremony. Thunder crashed about the stands, reverberating through the encircling pine forests of Lüneberg Heath. Huge straggling claws of electricity snatched at the charred sky as columns of rain plummeted to earth.

Two miles away Killaire stood alone in the stables. Maybe he was recollecting my mother saying to me earlier in the day, as Liz, his nanny, and I sat with him, 'Being mother to you is like being mother to a lightning conductor.'

Later that week the area of Killaire's injury was located somewhere in the foot. X-rays revealed nothing. The cause of lameness remained unobvious.

After his initial triumph when he was runner up at Burghley in 1976 Killaire gave me a watch from Garrards. I wore it all the time and was without it only when it was being engraved with one of Killaire's major three-day event successes.

Coincidentally, after Badminton 1979 there was still enough space for one more inscription. A few weeks before Luhmühlen the winder fell out. It was repaired in time for our trip. The morning we left for Germany the winder fell out of Killaire's watch again.

While I was hunting him in Leicestershire in January 1980, Be Fair, at the age of seventeen, landed too steeply over a hedge and ruptured nearly everything he could in his near foreleg. By June, it was apparent that his injury was deteriorating rather than improving, and his discomfort was increasing. On the advice of Nipper Constance, I decided that there was only one suitable place for Be Fair, and I asked my mother to have him put down while I was in Australia.

George hunted for several years after his Badminton and Burghley triumphs of 1977 and now lives in retirement with the Strakers in Yorkshire.

Killaire very nearly won Badminton for the second year in succession in 1980, but a mistake at the water jump on the final day relegated him to second place. He is, however, the only horse ever to have been first, second and third at Badminton.

He has since spent two years being the perfect schoolmaster to Emma Copeman, taking her through Juniors to Open Intermediates and Advanced one-day events. He is now semi-retired, doing the occasional hunter trial, and he appeared in splendid form as my mount for the parade of Equestrienne Personalities at the Horse of the Year Show in October 1984.

Appendix 1
INTERVAL TRAINING

Many people have asked me to write about interval training but it is not a subject which can be written down comprehensively. Even attempting to put it on paper may be unwise. Horses are not machines, and although it is perfectly possible to give a breakdown of how a tractor can be made to work the same does not apply to making a horse fit. A little knowledge is a dangerous thing, but I dare not give more than an outline of the basic principle:

Following the initial six weeks of road work, schooling and the general beginnings of toning and hardening up, the programme can commence. The objective is to enable a horse to reach his peak of fitness with the minimum amount of wear and tear. Accordingly training sessions, or work-outs, take place once every three or four days, gradually increasing the amount of canter work at each session. Apparently it takes between three and four days for a horse fully to recover from a work-out. To work a horse any sooner is to work a tired limb and invite injury; to work him later will benefit the horse correspondingly less as his muscles are beginning to slacken. If a horse is becoming too fit too soon, spacing the work-outs at five-, six- or even seven-day intervals will effectively slow up his progress.

The length of each of the three canters involved in each work-out and of the two intervening periods of relaxation and walking should be calculated to produce a horse almost fully recovered during the first break and half to threequarters recovered during the second. If he is asked to work again just before he has recovered he will thereby increasingly expand his heart and lung capacity thus building up his fitness in relation. This is a more logical approach than conventional fitness-training programmes which often involve pounding on in canter for twenty minutes or more at a time.

In 1974 when Bruce Davidson first introduced me to the system I worked from a pattern. Basically it began with three sessions of three-minute canters at 400 metres a minute interspersed with two three-minute breaks – 3 (3) 3 (3) 3 – and it built up over intervals of four days to three ten-minute canters at 400 metres a minute with two three-minute breaks between each – 10 (3) 10 (3) 10. It was only during the last three or four work-outs that any fast work was incorporated.

It is speed that kills. Galloping breaks down a horse quicker than any other work. During the last three or four work-outs of any training programme, four to five furlongs at a threequarter-speed gallop is about as much as I do.

Over the years I have come to appreciate how impossible it is to write a formula for fitness because every horse is different and requires slightly different work. It soon became evident that three lots of ten-minute canters involved too much hard work for my particular horses. The right amount depends on the type of horse, its temperament and the terrain being used. Flat terrain will require longer slow cantering than will hilly terrain. Hilly terrain is ideal for cold-blooded horses (e.g. Killaire, Badminton 1979). In this case the canters can be reduced to a total of maybe only seventeen or eighteen minutes.

These may be broken up into only two lots with accelerations uphill to keep the horse's incentive and interest. Fast work up not too steep an incline produces far less strain on the legs than it does when carried out on the flat. Also, less distance needs to be covered when galloping uphill. However, when canter work is carried out on hills, descents should be gradual and at an angle to lessen any jarring on the front legs. When the going is very hard it is advisable to canter uphill only.

The feeling required when developing a horse's fitness with slow work is the following: he must be pumping up against your hand and flexing his muscles every stride, not lolloping along. (Preferably not behaving like Gossip and fighting for freedom every stride, either.)

In preparation for Badminton 1979, Killaire's interval training programme began at the end of February. Given below are details of the last seven weeks leading up to Badminton.

MARCH

Tues	6th	5 (3) 5 (3) 5 – on the flat, at 400 m/min
		(i.e. 1 mile per 4 mins)
Sat	10th	6 (3) 6 (3) 6 – on the flat, at 400 m/min
Tues	13th	6 (3) 6 (3) 6 – on the flat, at 400 m/min
Sat	17th	7 (3) 6 (3) 7 – on the flat, at 400 m/min
Tues	20th	7 (3) 7 (3) 7 – on the flat, slightly faster canter:
		425–450 m/min
Sat	24th	8 (3) 6 (3) 8 – on the flat, slightly faster canter:
		425–450 m/min
Tues	27th	7 (3) 8 – on hills, including three spurts uphill
Sat	31st	Rushall One-Day Event

APRIL

Fri	6th	8 (2½) 7½ – on hills, including three spurts uphill
Wed	11th	9 (3) 8 – on hills, including four spurts uphill
Mon	16th	7 (2½) plus ¾ mile gallop – on the flat
Thurs	19th	Cantered up a hill
Fri	20th	Pipe-opener up a hill
Sat	21st	Cross-country day, Badminton

NB: This programme was designed specifically for a cold-blooded, fairly lazy horse. The intervening days are taken up with mostly walking and/or schooling. The day after each work-out should always be devoted either to a long walk or to resting.

Some horses will respond better to a progamme wherein the number of minutes they canter in any one bout never exceeds six, but instead the speed is gradually increased. A useful programme can be worked out whereby the last minute of the second and third canters can be increased to 500 metres per minute and 600 metres per minute respectively, starting approximately eight work-outs before the three-day event. This routine can be continued until the speed of the final minute of each of the last two canters has increased to 550 metres per minute and 650 metres per minute respectively.

Appendix 2
VITAL STATISTICS

BE FAIR
Owned by the author
Bred in Gloucestershire by Miss Joan Rymer
16.2 h.h. chestnut gelding
By FAIR AND SQUARE (three-day event horse)
Ex HAPPY REUNION (classically bred mare; believed raced
  and hunted)
Won Badminton 1973; age 10 years
Won European Championship (Luhmühlen) 1975; age 12
  years
Represented Great Britain at Montreal Olympics 1976; age
  13 years

WIDE AWAKE
Owned by Mrs V. Phillips
Bred in Oxfordshire by Mr and Mrs Charles Cope
16.1 h.h. bay gelding
By HEREWARD THE WAKE (Thoroughbred sire)
Ex SERENADE (three-day event mare)
Won Dutch International (Boekelo) 1975; age 9 years
Won Badminton 1976; age 10 years

GEORGE
Owned and bred in Yorkshire by Mrs H. Straker
16.2 h.h. bay gelding
By ST GEORG (Thoroughbred sire sold to Germany)
Ex WINNIFRITH (point-to-point and hunter mare)
Won Badminton 1977; age 12 years
Won European Championship (Burghley) 1977; age 12
  years

KILLAIRE
Owned by Mr C. A. Cyzer
Bred in Northern Ireland
16.3 h.h. bay gelding
By CARNATIC (Thoroughbred sire sold to Ireland)
Dam unknown
Second at Burghley 1976; age 8 years
Third at Badminton 1977; age 9 years
Third at Ledyard (USA) 1977; age 9 years
Won Badminton 1979; age 11 years
Second at Badminton 1980; age 12 years